101 FIVE-STRING BANJO TIPS

STUFF ALL THE PROS KNOW AND USE

BY FRED SOKOLOW

with editorial assistance by Ronny Schiff

All photos provided by Stewart-MacDonald, Elderly Instruments,
Deering Banjos, Gold Tone, and Lynn Sokolow

Recording Credits
Fred Sokolow: Banjo and vocals
Recorded and mixed at Sossity Sound by Michael Monagan

ISBN 978-1-4584-7992-1

HAL•LEONARD® CORPORATION

7777 W. BLUEMOUND RD. P.O. BOX 13819 MILWAUKEE, WI 53213

In Australia Contact:
Hal Leonard Australia Pty. Ltd.
4 Lentara Court
Cheltenham, Victoria, 3192 Australia
Email: ausadmin@halleonard.com.au

Visit Hal Leonard Online at
www.halleonard.com

INTRODUCTION

Nothing sounds like a banjo… except a banjo! If you're a fan of that sound, this volume is filled with musical shortcuts, historical facts, and everything else relevant to the world of banjo: how to select one, which strings or picks you need, to whom you should listen, and a run-down on all the different picking styles and tunings.

The five-string banjo has been called the only uniquely American instrument, despite the fact that it originated in Africa and was brought to the U.S. by slaves. In America, the banjo changed physically, eventually acquiring the snare drum-like head of the modern instrument. Today, you hear it in movie and TV car chases, country/western hits, commercials, bluegrass shows, and indie pop recordings. Recent Americana-style groups like the Avett Brothers, Mumford and Sons, and Old Crow Medicine Show (of "Wagon Wheel" fame) have caused a resurgence of interest in the five-string. But die-hard banjo people are used to these periodic episodes of banjomania.

In the early 1800s, minstrel banjo music took America and Europe by storm. Around the end of that century, minstrel was old hat, and the banjo was a more genteel parlor instrument suitable for classical tunes, ballads, and rags, likely as a piano to grace the middle class American home. By the 1920s, the five-string was mainly heard in old-time string band music of the South. After a few decades, interest in the instrument subsided, only to be renewed in the late 1940s by Earl Scruggs and the birth of bluegrass. Segue to the end of the 1950s, and banjo had become a leading voice in the urban folk revival. When rock all but eclipsed every other form of music, the banjo once again had a renaissance in the 1970s due to the "Dueling Banjos" scene in the movie *Deliverance*. After another dry spell, banjo bounced back, big-time, with the film *O Brother, Where Art Thou?* The jazz and classical innovations of Béla Fleck, along with the popular Steve Martin's return to his bluegrass banjo roots, didn't hurt either. Nor did Sufjan Stevens' use of the banjo, along with other indie artists and Americana groups.

And so it goes: banjo has its ups and downs, but it keeps evolving and coming back to capture people's ears and imaginations. If you're a banjo person, or you want to be, this book is for you. I've been a banjo person nearly all my life, so… welcome to the banjo world!

Keep picking,

Fred Sokolow

Fred Sokolow

ACKNOWLEDGMENTS

Thanks to Jody Stecher and Zac Sokolow for some arcane banjo lore, and thanks to Pete Seeger and Earl Scruggs, who brought me (and countless other happy pickers) to the banjo.

ABOUT THE AUTHOR

Fred Sokolow is best known as the author of over 150 instructional and transcription books and DVDs for guitar, banjo, Dobro, mandolin, and ukulele. Fred has long been a well-known West Coast multi-string performer and recording artist, particularly on the acoustic music scene. The diverse musical genres covered in his books and DVDs, along with several bluegrass, jazz, and rock albums he has released, demonstrate his mastery of many musical styles. Whether he's playing Delta bottleneck blues, bluegrass or old-time banjo, '30s swing guitar or screaming rock solos, he does it with authenticity and passion.

Fred's other banjo books include:

- *Fretboard Roadmaps: Five-String Banjo*
  (book/CD, Hal Leonard)

- *Complete Bluegrass Banjo*
  (book/CD, Hal Leonard)

- *Beatles for Banjo*
  (book/CD, Hal Leonard)

Email Fred with any questions about this or his other banjo books at: Sokolowmusic.com.

TABLE OF CONTENTS

PARTS OF THE BANJO

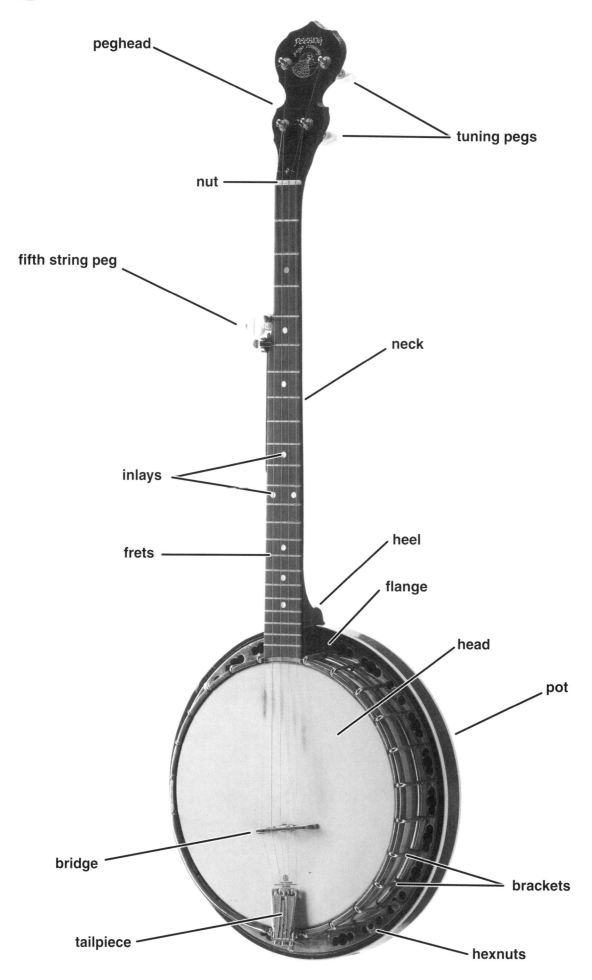

peghead

tuning pegs

nut

fifth string peg

neck

inlays

frets

heel

flange

head

pot

bridge

brackets

tailpiece

hexnuts

② RESONATOR VS. OPEN-BACKED

The resonator, made of wood, is often decorated on the back with wooden inlays. It makes the banjo louder and projects the sound outward, toward an audience or a microphone. If your banjo didn't come with a resonator, there are various ways to add one. They are usually attached to the flange, a metal hoop that encircles the head and holds the brackets. Sometimes it takes unscrewing about half a dozen Phillips-head screws to remove a resonator, but many of them are attached by four thumbscrews, which are hand-tightened (no tools needed to unscrew them).

Although you can play any kind of music on any banjo, it's a tradition that bluegrass players usually play banjos with resonators, and old-time banjoists tend to play open-backed banjos. Advantages of the open-backed banjo: 1. It's lighter! 2. You can stuff a pillow or small towel in the back of the banjo to muffle the sound, which is handy if you're practicing somewhere where it's disturbing neighbors, roommates, spouses, etc. Of course, you can remove a resonator and do the same thing.

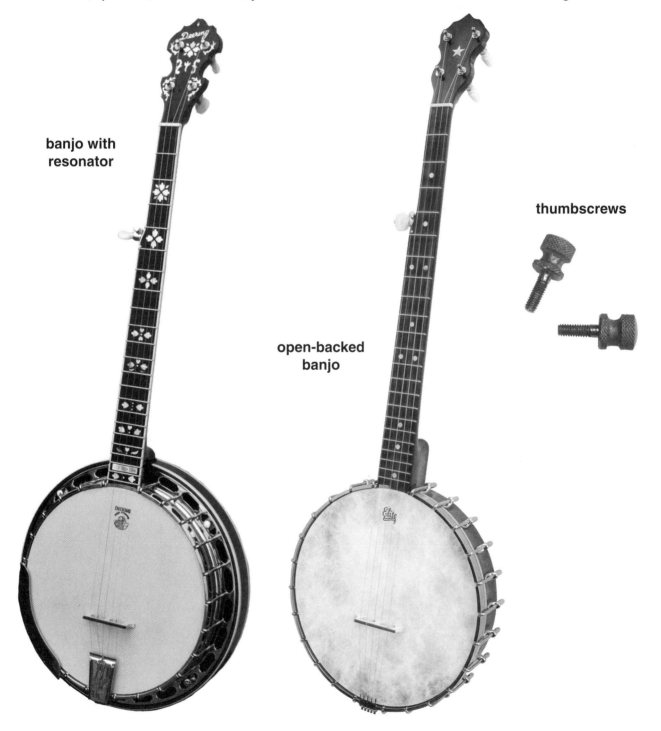

banjo with resonator

open-backed banjo

thumbscrews

3 GOURD BANJOS

Some of the first banjos were made by cutting open a large gourd and stretching an animal skin over it and tacking the skin to the sides. Then a neck was attached to this natural, organically grown resonating chamber. (The Indian sitar, among other instruments, is partly made from a gourd as well.) The early gourd banjos had fretless necks, strings made from woven vines, and friction pegs. Instruments fitting this description were seen in Africa, South America, and the West Indies as early as the 1600s. Sometimes calling them a *banjah*, *bandore*, or *banza*, many Europeans described similar instruments being played by American slaves. In 1781, Thomas Jefferson described the gourd banjos he saw slaves playing and said, "The instrument proper to them is the Banjar, which they brought hither from Africa, and which is the original of the guitar, its chords being precisely the four lower chords of the guitar."

Gourd banjos were also mentioned in descriptions of white settlers in the late 1700s on the frontier in Virginia, North Carolina, Kentucky, and many parts of Appalachia. But as banjos spread throughout the country, the wooden hoop-style banjo became standard, and gourd banjos became relics of a bygone era.

But not anymore! With just a few moments of Internet research, you can locate artisans and luthiers who are currently manufacturing gourd banjos in a very retro, pre-industrial style and selling them for reasonable prices. They're a lot of fun to play and have a unique sound.

4 MINSTREL BANJOS

Minstrel banjo music became a worldwide fad in the early 19th century, and it continued to grow until the end of the Civil War. The genre was characterized by white musicians in blackface, imitating the clawhammer (down-picking) banjo music of African Americans, along with a fiddle, tambourine, and bones (for percussion). Dancers were often part of the show as well. Minstrel banjoists played melodies with their index finger, using a thimble for a fingerpick, and their instruments were much like the early gourd banjos. They were fretless, with gut strings (or woven vines for strings), but they often had a wooden hoop rather than a gourd for the sound box. No brackets (no metal at all) were involved in the construction of minstrel banjos; they were all animal and vegetable—no minerals.

Joel Sweeney, often (erroneously) credited with inventing the five-string banjo (or adding the fifth string, or inventing the wooden hoop banjo), sparked the minstrel craze. In the 1820s, this young white Virginia farmer learned to play banjo from neighboring African Americans and was perhaps the first white man to perform with a banjo onstage. By the 1840s, he and his group had toured all over the South, New York, and Great Britain, where he played banjo for Queen Victoria. Other groups like the Virginia Minstrels and the Christy Minstrels helped expand the popularity of minstrel music, and it remained popular throughout the U.S. and Britain for most of the 19th century, exposing worldwide audiences of all races to the five-string banjo.

After the Civil War, banjo music started evolving in other directions, but the minstrel music craze helped bring the banjo, which had been largely an African/American instrument, to a huge white audience. Now minstrel is back (but without the charcoal/facial makeup)! Texts from "back in the day" document the tunings used, and many of the songs were written out in standard music notation. So, contemporary performers are reviving the music, and banjo makers are making minstrel banjos very similar to those of the minstrel era. You can see performances on YouTube and visit websites like minstrelbanjo.ning.com to learn all about past and present minstrel banjo. You can see some beautiful instruments on minstrelbanjo.com.

5 THE FIFTH (DRONE) STRING

In old American literature about the banjo, circa the 18th and 19th centuries, the fifth string was called the *chanterelle*. Some of the earliest paintings and drawings of American banjos indicate that they had a short, high-pitched fifth string with a tuning peg halfway up the neck that pre-dated the four-string banjo and Joel Sweeney (who claimed to have added the fifth string in the 19th century), and were probably derived from an African instrument.

The fifth string is rarely fretted, except in very advanced, up-the-neck, virtuoso picking, so that one droning, high note keeps ringing out throughout a song—even though the tune may have many chord changes. Hence, we have all the early American songs about hearing the banjo *ring*. Many instruments in other cultures have drone strings, such as the Indian sitar, but the banjo is the only popular American instrument with this feature.

There are many banjo tunings, but in most of them the fifth string is tuned to one of the three notes that comprise the tonic chord. In other words, if you tune to G or C, tune the fifth string to a G note, which is part of a G and a C chord. In D tuning, the fifth string is tuned to A or F♯, both of which are notes in a D major chord.

In most sets of banjo strings, the fifth string is the same gauge (thickness) as the first string. The fifth string is nearly always plucked by the thumb and not the fingers.

6 TUNING PEGS

There are basically two types of tuners, or tuning pegs:

- **Friction Pegs:** These have no gears; what you turn is what you get. These are the old-time tuners, and in their most primitive form, they resemble wooden violin tuning pegs.

- **Geared Pegs:** These are the more modern design and much easier to use. The geared fifth string is especially handy, as the drone string requires more tuning than the other four strings. This is especially true for bluegrass players who usually play in open G tuning but use a capo.

If you prefer a retro look but appreciate the benefits of modern technology, you can buy faux friction pegs that look like the oldest wooden pegs, but have hidden gears and tune very smoothly. They're perfect for a gourd or minstrel banjo that's difficult to tune!

friction peg   **two types of geared pegs**   **non-geared and geared 5th string peg**

7 ACTION

The distance between the strings and the fretboard is often referred to as the *action*. High action makes it harder to fret the strings, but if the action is too low, the strings will buzz or rattle against the frets when you bear down and pick hard. The trick is to get the action just right for your style of playing.

There are various ways to alter the action. You can raise it by switching to a higher bridge or tightening up the head. You can lower it by using a lower bridge or, sometimes, by deepening the notches in the nut. On some banjos, you can lower the action by adjusting the coordinating rods, which changes the angle of the neck in relation to the pot. If the banjo has a truss rod, it can be adjusted to straighten a warped neck, which also can affect action. You should consult your neighborhood music store rather than attempt this yourself, unless you're willing to do a lot of preliminary research! There are numerous illustrated articles on the subject online, as well as YouTube videos. See Tip #16 for more on truss rods and coordinating rods.

You can also lower the action on a banjo that lacks a truss rod or coordinating rods by putting a *shim* between the neck and the pot, as shown in the illustration below. Do some Internet research before attempting this!

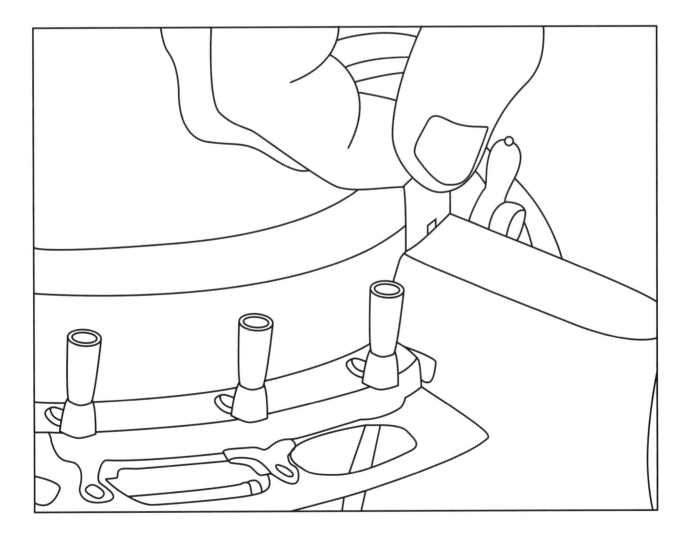

BANJO HEADS (SKIN, PLASTIC, FIBER)

Animal skins or vellums have been used on musical instruments (strings and percussion) for centuries in many cultures. In rural areas where early banjos were homemade, any animal skin might be used: rabbit, possum, sheep—you name it. By the end of the 19th century, calfskin was the standard vellum for manufactured instruments. This changed around the end of the 1950s when plastic heads became available and were immediately accepted by the banjo community (as well as the world of drummers).

Plastic heads are easy to install, and they are not as affected by weather and humidity changes as skin heads. This makes them considerably more trouble-free. They also give a banjo a brighter, crisper tone. Most plastic heads on banjos and drums are painted with a white exterior, often textured (frosted) to resemble the old-style heads, but some are clear, see-through plastic. The frost-free, clear heads have the brightest, crispest tone.

Still, many folks prefer the tubbier, more organic sound of animal skins. It's a living, breathing, organic membrane! Earl Scruggs recorded the original "Foggy Mountain Breakdown" with a calfskin banjo head!

The fiber head is a compromise. It simulates the sound and look of a skin head without the extra trouble. News flash! In recent years, Gold Tone has been offering a goatskin banjo head that is easy to install and relatively trouble-free… and it has that tubby sound favored by folks who believe that most banjos do not lack for high-end sounds. For aficionados of the older banjo sound, goatskin heads are great for banjos (bad news for goats, though).

By the way, skin heads and frosted plastic heads get worn where the picking hand makes the most contact. You can tell by the shape of the wear whether the player is a fingerpicker or "clawhammerer" (see illustrations).

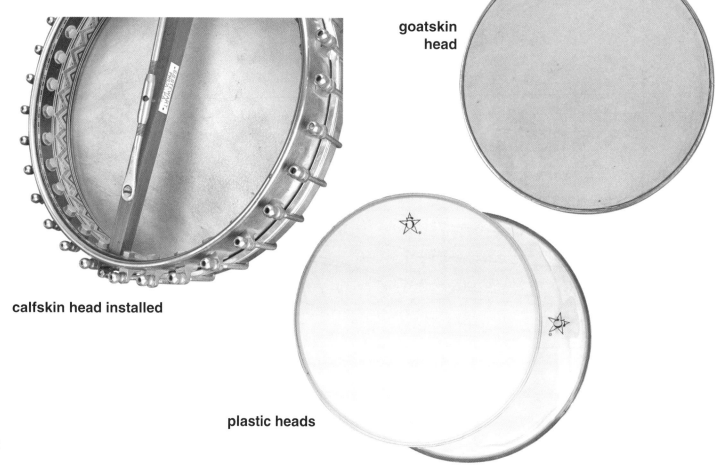

goatskin head

calfskin head installed

plastic heads

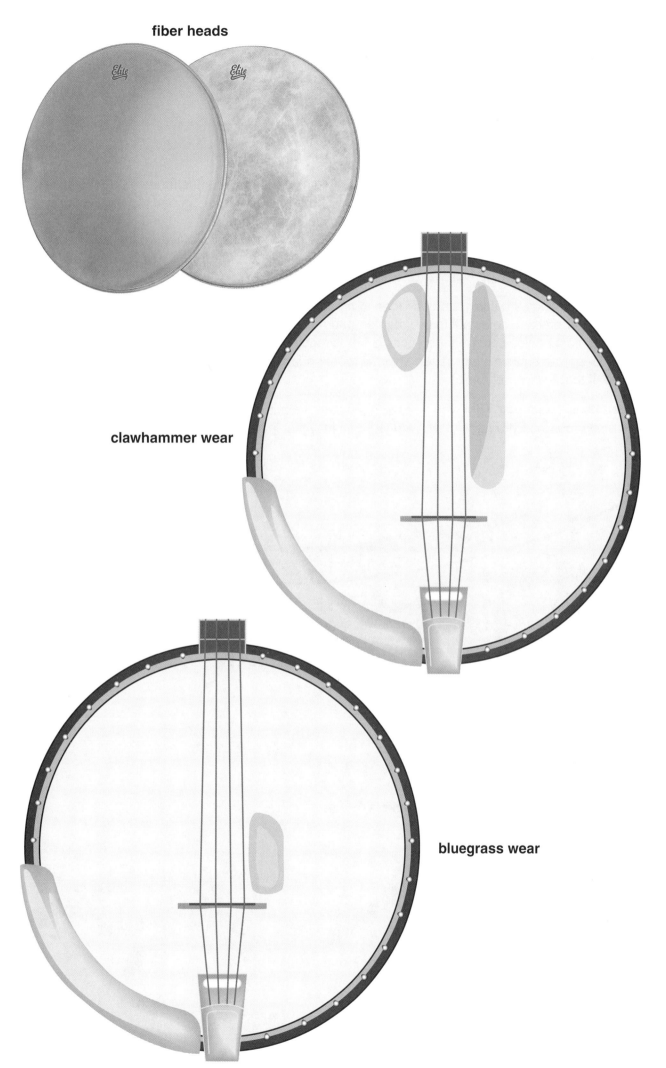

fiber heads

clawhammer wear

bluegrass wear

13

9 TIGHTENING THE HEAD (BRACKETS)

A tight banjo head is a plus (brighter tone and more volume), so better instruments tend to have more brackets (or hooks). Typically, there are 16–24 brackets that hook around the metal tension hoop that encircles the banjo head. Tighten the hexnuts on the brackets and you pull the hoop down, tightening the head. When it's tight enough, the bridge doesn't cause a depression in the head; it sits flat on the head. A tight banjo head makes a bright sound when you thump or tap the head with your index fingernail.

When you first buy a banjo, it's a good idea to tighten up the head. Do this slowly at first, an eighth of a turn per bracket, so as not to over tighten and rip the head. The hexnuts on brackets vary in size, but most banjos come with the appropriate wrench, and various wrenches can be bought at banjo-oriented music stores. Then again, a looser head gives your banjo a warmer, more retro sound, if that's your preference.

If your banjo has a resonator, you need to remove it to reach the brackets. As mentioned in Tip #2, this may require a Phillips-head screwdriver, or it may just involve loosening four thumbscrews.

brackets installed

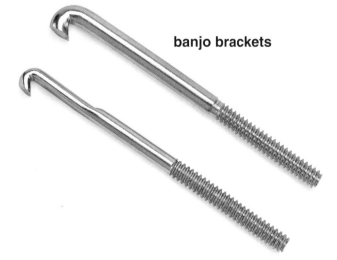

banjo brackets

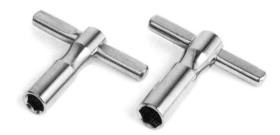

banjo wrenches

10 TONE RINGS

In better-made banjos, the plastic or skin head rests on a metal tone ring, which is made of brass, bronze, or any number of alloys. The tone ring, which adds several pounds to the weight of the banjo, rests on the wooden rim. If the banjo has no tone ring, the head sits directly on the wooden or metal rim.

There is a world of controversy about tone rings: which metals should be used? Which shape? One piece or two or more pieces welded together? How, exactly, do they work?

But it all comes down to listening to different banjos with different types of tone rings and deciding for yourself which sound you prefer. Check out the Deering Banjo website for some background and clarification of the issues involved.

About a century ago, the Gibson Company standardized their Mastertone ring, which is a one-piece cast bronze ring that weighs about three pounds. Many bluegrass banjo pickers still consider this the preferred tone ring.

Around 1909, the Vega Company made a Tubaphone model banjo, highly prized and now imitated by other companies. It had a distinctive tone ring made of several sections welded together with holes in it (see photo), which were visible, as these were open-backed banjos. Old-time pickers still prize the Tubaphone banjos, and many fine banjo makers imitate the Tubaphone tone ring.

flat top tone ring

arch top tone ring

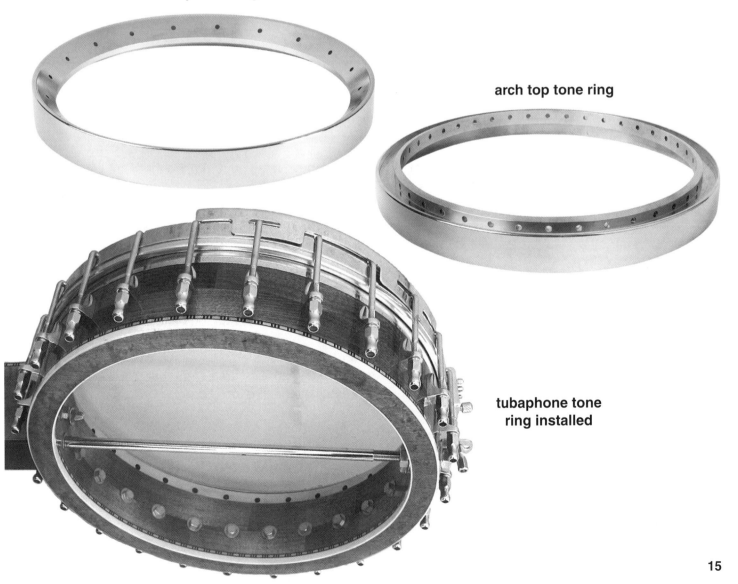

tubaphone tone ring installed

11 THE BRIDGE

The banjo bridge is not attached to the banjo head. String tension holds it in place, so it comes off when you take off the banjo strings. Many people make a pencil mark on the banjo head to help them relocate the bridge in the right position after changing strings.

There are many varieties of bridges, but they're all made of wood, and most have two or three feet that sit on the banjo head. Since the bridge transmits string vibrations to the banjo head, it's crucial to the sound of the instrument. (Pick some open strings while holding the bridge between your thumb and finger, and the sound will be extremely muted.) The strings fit into notches that are carved on the top of the bridge. If the notches are too shallow, the string may fly out of its notch when you pick hard. If the notch is too deep, the string may rattle audibly.

To position the bridge properly, move it around until a note that is plucked while fretted at the 12th fret sounds exactly like the 12th fret harmonic (see Tip #44 on harmonics). If the fretted note is sharp, move the bridge back toward the tailpiece. If it's flat, move the bridge forward, away from the tailpiece.

12 ARCH TOP VS. FLAT TOP

flat top

arch top

There are two types of tone rings (see Tip #10), and they determine whether a banjo is an arch top or flat top:

- Flat top tone rings have a tall outer rim, so the head lies flat (see top photo).

- The arch top tone ring has a taller inner ring and a shorter outer ring, so the head has a raised (arched) inner circle, as shown in the bottom photo.

Arch top banjos have a brighter, crisper tone and less bass response—there's a lot of high end on these banjos! Ralph Stanley always played arch tops and was famous for his icy, brittle tone. Flat top banjos have a balanced tone with more mids and bass, presumably because of the larger vibrating surface area of the head. Earl Scruggs always played a flat top Gibson.

 13 ARMREST

Many banjos come with an armrest. If yours does not, they can be purchased separately and are easy to install. There are several shapes and sizes of armrest, but they all do the same thing: they attach to the brackets near the tailpiece and protect your wrist or upper arm from being irritated or bruised by the brackets. When you rest your wrist directly on the banjo, the brackets leave marks or welts.

Vega armrest

Mastertone armrest

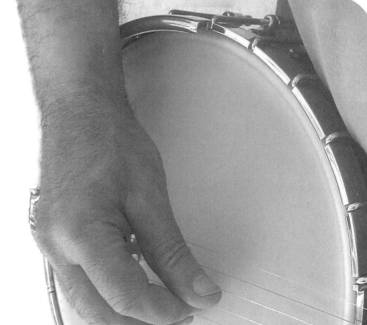

armrest installed

 14 FRETLESS BANJOS

As mentioned in Tips #3 and #4, early banjos were fretless. Not only the minstrel style, but also Appalachian and other old-time banjo styles were developed on fretless banjos, and many pickers still prefer them— especially folks who enjoy recreating older banjo sounds. The sliding sound of a fretless banjo is unique, whether the strings are nylon, gut, or steel. Most fretless players confine their playing to the first five or six "frets."

After the Civil War, there was a trend toward more sophisticated banjo music. Some people considered the minstrel style primitive, and they preferred fingerpicking to the downstroke (clawhammer) style. In the 1870s, some banjo makers installed strips of wood or bone, flush with the fingerboard, to help players find notes farther up the neck. Around the same time, two popular minstrel banjoists, James Buckley and Frank Converse, published instruction books that taught fingerpicking. Buckley included instructions on how to install actual fretwires (like guitar frets) on your banjo. Finally, in the early 1880s, a famous banjo player and maker named Henry Dobson began manufacturing fretted banjos. It was all part of a movement to legitimize the instrument, and by the end of the 19th century, some banjoists with fretted instruments (and gut strings) played first-violin parts and fronted classical orchestras—a far cry from the minstrel shows of olden days!

Today most banjos are fretted, and bluegrass is always played on fretted banjos.

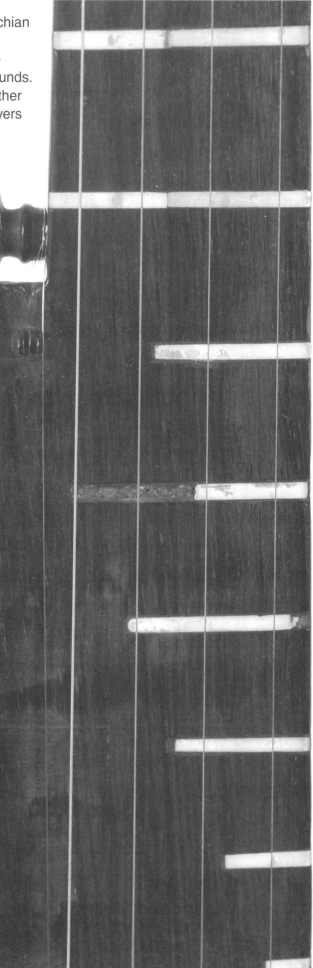

inlaid fake frets

15 INLAYS

Inlays are the pearl or abalone dots, trapezoids, or elaborate designs carved into the banjo fretboard. These are both for decoration and to help the picker find his or her way around the neck. Most banjos have some kind of marking at the 5th, 7th, 9th, and 12th frets, at the very least, as these are critical and often used position markers.

The inlay patterns on pegheads can be very ornate as well, and these serve no useful purpose other than making the banjo beautiful. Often the peghead inlay includes the name of the manufacturer (Gibson, Paramount, Wildwood, etc.) and even the name of the model ("style A").

Beyond their utilitarian purpose, inlays make a simple banjo look fancy. Many pre-war Gibson banjos had very ornate inlay patterns that have since become widely imitated and have been dubbed with colorful names like "hearts and flowers," "flying eagle," "gulls and bows," "diamonds and squares," and "wreath," to name just a few. Inlaying can be quite an art, as the pictures below attest.

16 COORDINATING/TRUSS RODS

If your banjo's action is higher than you like (see Tip #7), and a lower bridge or loosened head is not an option, you may need to make adjustments to your coordinating rods—if your banjo has them, that is! Better banjos have two coordinating rods inside the pot. They're visible on an open back banjo, or they're exposed when you remove a resonator. The rods are adjustable; they change the neck angle, and therefore they raise or lower the action.

If you adjust the rods to make the neck tilt down, the action is lowered. As mentioned in Tip #7, there are numerous online, illustrated discussions of how and when to make these adjustments. Sometimes they are described under the headings "banjo setup" or "setting up your banjo." Your local music store can also take care of it.

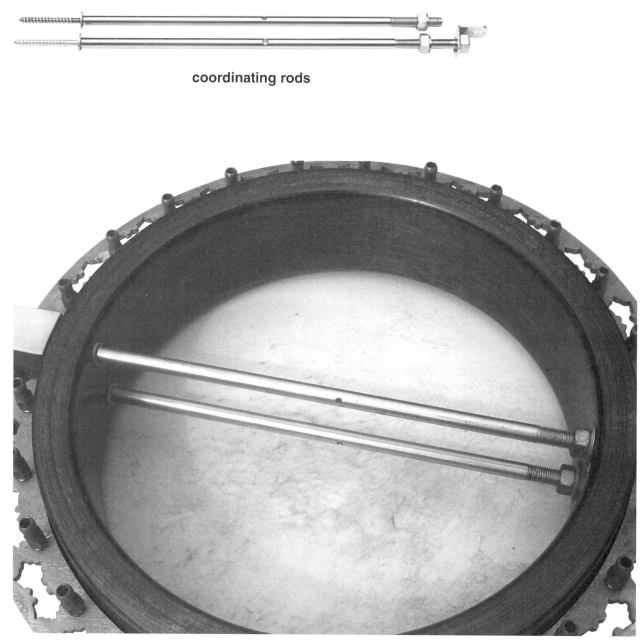

coordinating rods

coordinating rods installed

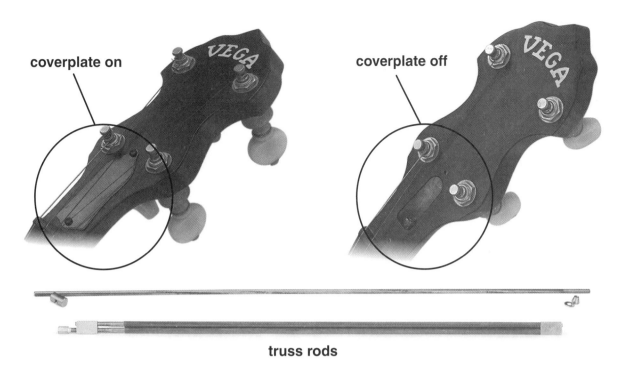

coverplate on coverplate off

truss rods

If your banjo's neck is warped, or if you have string buzzing that isn't caused by uneven frets, you may need to adjust your truss rod—again, if your banjo has one. Many banjos have a metal pole inside the banjo's neck that extends the length of the neck. If your banjo has a truss rod, there's a cover plate on the peghead, probably made of plastic, that conceals an adjusting nut.

By turning the adjusting nut, you can alter the curve of the neck to correct for high action or warpage that causes strings to buzz. Online articles or videos on how to do this may be listed under "banjo neck relief" or "banjo setup."

17 SELECTING A BANJO

Get the best banjo you can afford. Consider that the better the instrument, the easier it is to play, and the quicker you'll improve. Plus, if you're excited about your banjo every time you open the case, you'll spend more time with it and advance more quickly.

Go somewhere you can try out several different banjos, and when you do, here's what to look for:

- Is it easy to fret? Does the fingerboard feel comfortable when you fret chords on it?

- Is the neck straight? Sight down the neck as if through a gunsight.

- Is the neck too thick? Some necks are harder to get your hand around than others.

- Is the fretboard too narrow for your fingers when you're playing a chord?

- Does it have a good sound, compared to other banjos you've played?

- Do you like the way it looks?

The open back versus resonator issue is not important unless you plan to play professionally in a bluegrass band, in which case you probably want a resonator.

Deering and Gold Tone make inexpensive banjos that are stripped down (no frills) but have well-made necks and are good for beginners.

The tuning pegs that stick out on the sides are not as well made or easy to tune with as the ones that stick out behind the peghead.

PRACTICE WITH A METRONOME

If you discover while playing with other people or with recordings that your rhythm is erratic (you get out of synch with others), practice with a metronome.

A *metronome* is a mechanical or digital device that keeps time by emitting rhythmic clicks or beeps at variable, measurable speeds. It forces you to keep a steady tempo! You can set your metronome to whatever slow, medium, or fast speed suits you. Musicians have used the metronome for centuries as a practice aid. Its numerical settings are standard throughout the world (beats per minute or "bpm") and are often noted on written music to indicate the preferred tempo of a piece.

If you wander off the beat by speeding up or slowing down, those insistent ticks, tocks, clicks, or beeps make it impossible to ignore your error. You can buy inexpensive metronomes, and there are several free ones online, as well as smart phone apps.

19 GET ORGANIZED

Keep it all together—in a binder: Random scraps of paper won't do! Have a music binder or folder containing all the songs and exercises on which you're working, as well as all the tunes you already know. Add your repertoire list. Carry it with you everywhere you go with the banjo—to jam sessions, music lessons, the park, friends' houses, etc. Alphabetize the songs so you can find them easily!

Build up a set list: Make a list of songs you can play all the way through. You're building up a repertoire. Keep the list in your banjo case. You'll need it at jam sessions and at Carnegie Hall. Your list should include the key in which you like to play and sing each song. It doesn't matter how easy or impressively difficult they are; just list songs you like and can play. Even if you can't play a solo on a song, if you know how it goes and know the chord changes, put it on the list. If you can sing it, so much the better!

Get a music stand: When you're reading music from songbooks (to follow the lyrics, the chords, or the music), you need a stand; it beats balancing a book in your lap. Some music stands fold up and are portable, but they're not as stable as the solid stands. There are also desktop stands.

Many banjo players use two fingerpicks and a thumbpick. The fingerpicks are usually metal and bendable, so one size fits all. The thumbpicks, usually plastic, come in different sizes. All bluegrass players use these, and many two-finger pickers also wear them. Clawhammer players usually use their index fingernail and no picks, although some use a backwards fingerpick to make the melody notes stand out (see photo, below).

Picks feel awkward when you first use them; there's a learning curve. But they make your banjo louder and clearer, which is important if you perform or jam with other players. Picking hard for any length of time with your bare fingers makes them sore.

fingerpicks & thumbpick

backwards fingerpick

HOW TO USE A STRAP

Many people find straps essential. They give you freedom (you don't have to hold up the banjo while playing it) and security.

- Your local music store or (or internet music store) offers banjo straps of many materials, colors, and sizes. Most of them are adjustable to fit taller or shorter pickers.

- Banjo straps are usually attached to two brackets: the one near the tailpiece and the one nearest the neck (see illustration).

- Some straps include metal or plastic clips that attach to the brackets, while others have strings or strips of leather or rawhide that tie around the brackets.

- Many players put the strap on one shoulder; others put it around their neck (see photos). The one-shoulder arrangement makes it easier to pick up the instrument and put it down in a hurry, which is handy in a performance if you switch instruments. Earl Scruggs wore it that way (which makes it, by definition, the proper way to wear it!).

AMPLIFYING YOUR BANJO

You get the most natural, amplified banjo sound by playing into a microphone that's connected to an amplifier or a P.A. system. This limits your motion; you have to stick right by the microphone—so no choreography! Here are some alternative ways to amplify as well:

miniature microphone (mini-mic)

- Many companies make a miniature mic, which can be mounted on a gooseneck that is attached to your banjo, pointed right at the sweet spot—the place where your banjo emits the best tone. Some of these mini mics plug into a preamp box on the floor with knobs to adjust tone and volume. Or, you can go wireless.

- Pickups, or transducers, are less expensive and less plagued with feedback problems than mini-mics. The pickups can be mounted on the banjo head or inside the pot. Some do not require a preamp. There are two types of pickups: piezo and magnetic. Some say piezo pickups make your banjo tone harsh and have feedback problems. But they are in wide use. They're easy to install, convenient, and inexpensive. Magnetic pickups are more expensive, but they create less feedback problems and many say they render a more natural sound than piezo.

Many of the banjo makers listed in Tip #97 sell amplifying systems and discuss the issues at length. Janet Davis's Acoustic Music website sells and describes many different types of mini mics and pickups. Go to your local music store and try some out.

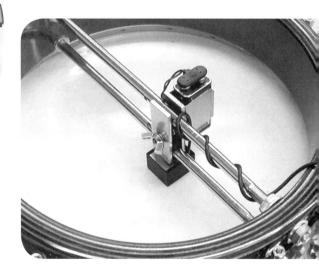

EMG magnetic pickup   **Fishman magnetic pickup**

23 FINGERNAILS

Keep the fingernails of your fretting hand very short, as it's hard to fret the strings cleanly with long nails (only Dolly Parton can play a banjo with long nails).

If you wear fingerpicks on your picking hand, nails are not an issue. But clawhammer banjoists have at least one long fingernail on their picking hand. Depending on which finger you use for melody notes, the index fingernail or the middle fingernail need some length to get a clear, loud note when you're down-picking. Some people even reinforce that nail with a false fingernail.

24 THERE'S AN APP FOR THAT

Apps for banjos abound. Tuning apps are especially helpful. Banjo apps are available for all different gizmos from your smartphone to your tablets. Many have chord dictionaries, fretboard configurations, strumming patterns, instruction, songbooks, etc. Be sure to read reviews, as some of them seem to be in a perpetual "beta" stage and not realized enough.

25 JUST IN CASE (BANJO CASES)

Obviously, you want to protect your banjo. When purchasing a case, consider your lifestyle (traveling around or playing at home), the value of your banjo (monetary and sheer love), and the size and shape of your banjo. Look for a lot of pockets as well. If you're ordering online, be sure to measure your banjo.

- **Hard Shell Cases**: The basic ones have a bit of internal padding and a good handle; the fanciest have pockets, super padding, waterproofing, and scuff-resistant outside edges. Most are made of wood or metal.

- **Hard Foam Cases**: Constructed of hard foam and nylon, these are shaped like a hard shell case. They're lighter and easier to carry.

- **Soft Cases/Gig Bags**: More reasonably priced, but not as protective, soft cases are usually made out of heavy-duty (usually waterproofed), synthetic fabric. The better ones come with dense foam padding and have an adjustable backstrap and handle. Look for fit, padding, and an industrial-grade plastic zipper that won't scratch your instrument.

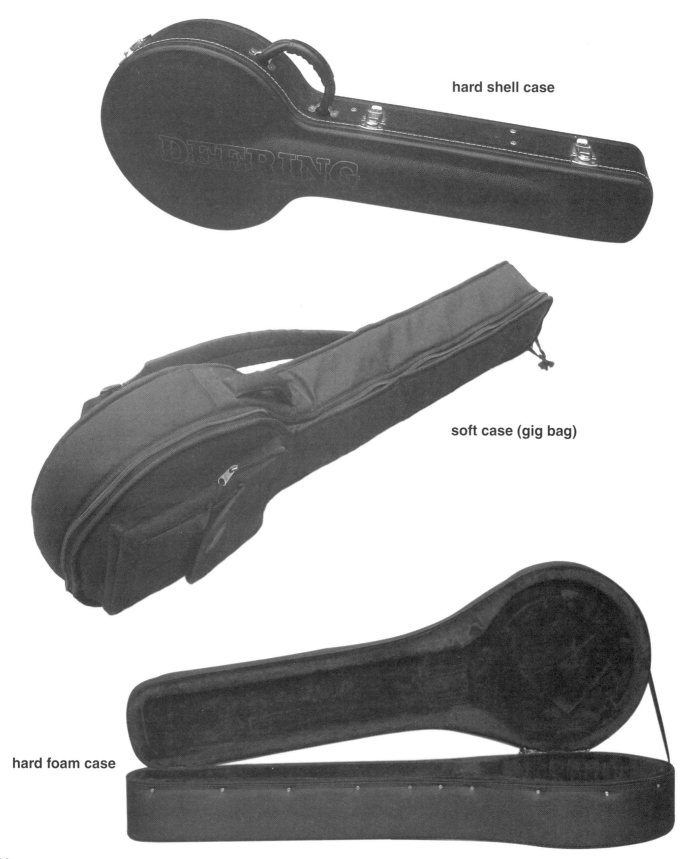

hard shell case

soft case (gig bag)

hard foam case

 STRINGS

Banjo strings seem to have evolved from vegetable vines to gut, nylon, and metal. Though some pickers prefer retro styles, the modern metal strings are by far the most widely used and easiest-to-find strings today. All bluegrassers and most old-time and folk banjoists use metal strings.

Some music stores sell metal banjo string sets of various gauges (thicknesses): heavy, medium, and light gauge. In all three sets, the fourth string is steel with a metal winding to make it thicker; the other four strings are unwound steel. Usually, the first and fifth strings are identical gauges. Light strings are easier on the fretting fingers, but medium gauge strings sound better. And, if you pick or strum really hard, you might want to try a heavier gauge set. If you can't find a heavy gauge set, you can create one out of single strings (if you can buy single strings at your local music store).

If you play a bit every day, you should change strings once a month. After a while, they won't stay in tune, and up-the-neck notes will be flat. If strings start to feel tarnished or rusty, they should have been changed long ago! Ditto if the wound fourth string starts to unwind.

It's possible to buy nylon strings for a retro classical, old-time, or ragtime banjo sound. Real gut strings are sold and often advertised as minstrel banjo strings, and "nylgut" strings are also available. They simulate the sound and feel of gut strings, but are not as susceptible to weather changes and are more durable.

 CAPOS

Originally called a *capo d'astro*, it has also been dubbed a cheater, or a crutch, but it's not fair to malign the capo. The list of players known to use one includes nearly every bluegrass banjo player (except Don Reno) and most old-time pickers and strummers, as well as folk musicians like Pete Seeger.

Using a capo, you can play in multiple keys without playing many barred chords. It's easier to get that clear, ringing tone with open strings than fretted ones, and that's where the capo comes in handy. It also makes difficult keys easier. The capo clamps down on all four strings (unless it's above the 5th fret, clamping down on all five), rendering the frets behind the capo useless. That's the only disadvantage of the capo; when you use it, you lose some low notes.

If your banjo is tuned to open G and you want to play in the key of A, place the capo at the 2nd fret. Then tune the fifth string up two frets higher than usual to match the capo (which is two frets higher than usual). Now, when you strum the open strings, you're playing an A chord instead of a G. Your C chord formation is now a D chord (two frets higher than C), D7 is now E7, and so on.

Here are some capo options for playing in G tuning, in keys other than G or C:

Key	Capo at this fret	Play as if you were in	Tune fifth string to
A♭	1	G	A♭ (G♯)
A	2	G	A
B♭	3	G	B♭
B	4	G	B
C♯	1	C	G♯
D	2	C	A
E♭	3	C	B♭ or G
E	4	C	B or G♯
F	5	C	C or A
F♯	6	C	C♯ or A♯

The fifth string is tuned to one of the notes in the I chord. For example, to play in E, retune the fifth string to G♯ or B. Both notes are in an E chord.

There are other ways to play in these keys, without a capo, but that's for a different Tip.

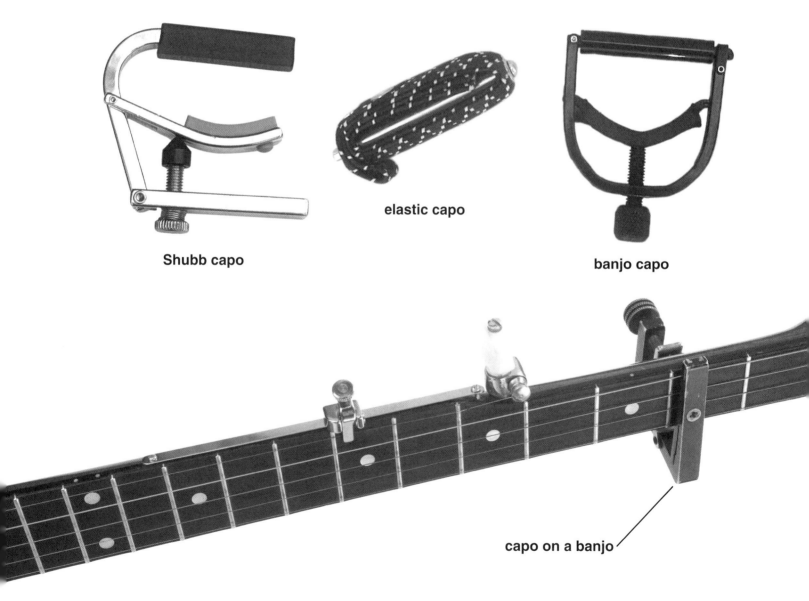

Shubb capo

elastic capo

banjo capo

capo on a banjo

Fifth string spikes (or capo spikes) are little L-shaped nails that are really spikes from an HO railroad set. You, or someone at a music store, nail them into your banjo fretboard at strategic spots, such as the 7th, 9th, and 10th frets (there are YouTube videos demonstrating how to install fifth string spikes). Then, when playing in keys other than G or C, you slip the fifth string under the nail, and its pitch is raised just the right amount. Sometimes a touch of fine-tuning is required.

For example, to play in the keys of A or D, instead of tuning the fifth string up to A, you slip it under the 7th fret spike. Now the open (unfretted) fifth string is an A note.

fifth string spikes

fifth string spikes installed

The fifth string capo is often preferred to the spike system by bluegrassers, because it's a bit faster to use and usually requires no fine tuning. A bar is installed atop the fretboard, and you slide a little hook apparatus up or down the bar, to the desired fret. The "hook" frets the fifth string, as shown below:

fifth string capo

There are a few disadvantages to the fifth string capo:

- Cosmetic—there's this metal contraption fastened to your banjo neck.

- Some people occasionally use their thumb to fret the fifth string, and they find that the bar gets in their way.

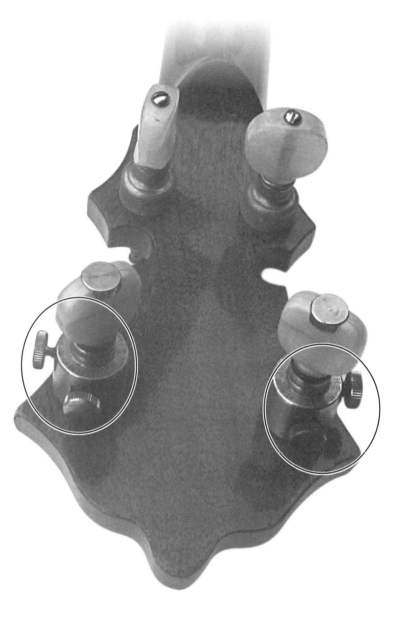

In the early 1950s, Earl Scruggs figured out a way to switch back and forth from G tuning to D tuning in the middle of a song (see Tips #30 and #32) without dropping a beat. He wrote instrumentals like "Earl's Breakdown," "Flinthill Special," and "Foggy Mountain Chimes" that featured a twangy detuning of the second and third strings, in mid-flight.

Scruggs built his tuners out of alarm clock parts and drilled two holes in his peghead, between the usual pegs, in which he installed normal tuning pegs augmented with cams that stuck out a fraction of an inch. When turned one way, the pegs "pushed in" on the third and second strings, raising their pitch. When turned the other way, they released the strings to their D tuning notes. Soon other bluegrass pickers began making and installing "Scruggs Tuners" on their banjos.

In 1963, Bill Keith invented a geared peg with controls (knobs) that made it stop at the desired high and low notes. These "Keith Pegs" replaced the second and third string pegs, and looked like normal banjo tuning pegs, so they were cosmetically better than Scruggs tuners, easier to install, and didn't require major banjo surgery. Many bluegrassers use them to this day.

Track 1 on the next page is an excerpt from "Home Sweet Home," played in D tuning (see Tip #33 for more on this tuning). It demonstrates how the tuners sound. (See Tip #75 for reading "Tablature.")

Home Sweet Home

D tuning (f♯DF♯AD)

Scruggs style

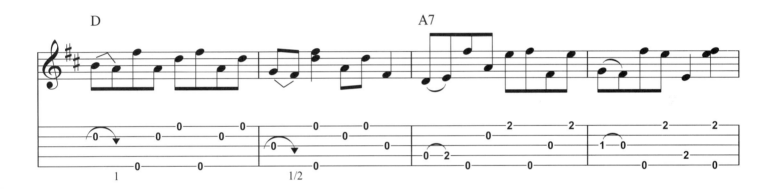

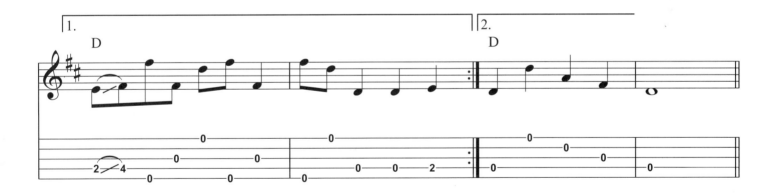

 **G TUNING**

Although five-string banjo players use many tunings, G tuning is today's most-used tuning, especially for bluegrass pickers. It's an open G chord; if you strum the unfretted banjo strings in this tuning, you're playing a G major chord: **gDGBD**.

TRACK 2

G Tuning:

5 = G

4 = D

3 = G

2 = B

1 = D

Here are some common banjo chord shapes, both first position and moveable chords (which can be played all over the fretboard):

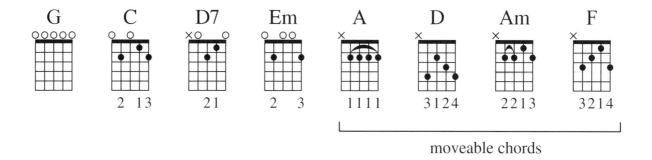

moveable chords

G tuning probably didn't gain much traction among banjo pickers until the end of the 19th century. Several banjo instruction books, starting with Briggs' 1855 *Banjo Instructor*, offered some songs in dADF♯A, which is an open D tuning, but the intervals are the same as G tuning, five frets lower. This was a variant of dGDF♯A, which is the predecessor of the C tuning (see Tip #35). Most classical banjo music, circa 1900, was written for C tuning, but some seems to be intended for G tuning.

It's interesting to note that the banjo G tuning nearly duplicates the old Mississippi Delta G tuning used by many African/American bottleneck blues guitar players. Considering that both blues and banjo come from Africa, or from African/Americans, there may be a connection here.

31 STAY TUNED!

Use an electronic tuner. There are many good, inexpensive ones on the market these days. The easiest ones to use clip right onto your banjo's headstock. Here are some other varieties. Some of these are available as apps for your phone and are free on websites:

- **Chromatic Tuners**: Stand alone tuners that can tune all 12 notes of the scale.

- **Pedal Tuners**: Rest on the floor with a pick-up mic wired directly to your banjo.

- **Pocket Strobe Tuners**: Have a strobe light display rather than a needle to indicate pitch.

Always pluck the string you're tuning as you're turning the tuning peg.

If you get a G note from a tuning fork, pitch pipe, piano, or some other instrument that you know is in proper tune, you can use the time-honored string-to-string method to tune your banjo. For G tuning:

- Tune the open G/third string to the fork/piano/whatever.

- Fret the G/third string at the 4th fret. Match the open B/second string to this note.

- Fret the B/second string at the 3rd fret. Match the open D/first string to this note.

- Fret the D/first string at the 5th fret. Match the open high G/fifth string to this note.

- Fret the D/fourth string at the 5th fret. Tune it to match the open G/third string.

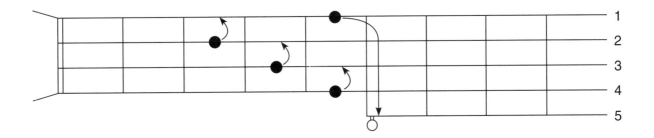

32  WHAT KEY ARE WE IN?

A *key* is like a sonic home base. If you're in the key of C, the song's melody is probably based on a C major scale, and the song feels at rest when you play the C chord. Leaving the C chord and going anywhere else causes varying degrees of tension, which you resolve by coming back to the C chord.

Here are some tips on figuring out a song's key by listening (something you need to do in order to play along with a recording, as in Tip #59):

- It's not always the first chord in the song, but it usually is the last chord.

- If a song fades out (so there's no final chord), listen for the "resolving" chord—the chord you could end the song on.

- Play one of the three moveable major chords (see Tip #42) and move it up the neck until it matches the resolving chord. If you don't find it by the 7th fret, switch to a different moveable chord.

33 D TUNING

The D tuning has long been used by old-time banjoists, and Scruggs' banjo style began to gel when, at the age of 10, he discovered a way to play "Reuben's Train" with three fingers in D tuning! Called "open D" because it tunes the banjo to an open (unfretted) D major chord, the tuning is **f♯DF♯AD**. Listen to it on Track #3:

TRACK 3

D Tuning:

5 = F♯

4 = D

3 = F♯

2 = A

1 = D

Some people tune the fifth string up to A, instead of down to F♯. D tuning duplicates the top four strings of the very popular "open D" guitar tuning used by many blues and slide players. Here are some D tuning chord shapes:

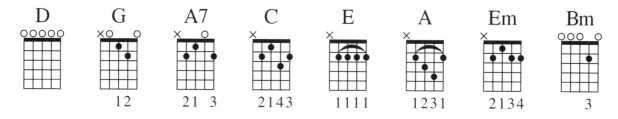

D tuning chords resemble G tuning chords "moved up a string." For instance:

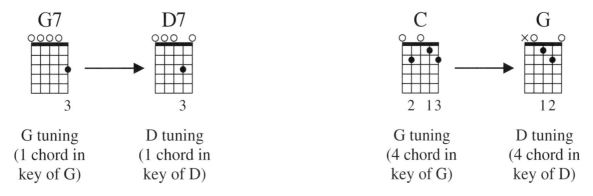

G7
G tuning
(1 chord in
key of G)

D7
D tuning
(1 chord in
key of D)

C
G tuning
(4 chord in
key of G)

G
D tuning
(4 chord in
key of D)

See Tip #80 for more on 1 chords and 5 chords.

D tuning bluegrass standards include Scruggs' "John Henry" and "Cora Is Gone," Don Reno's "Home, Sweet Home," and Ralph Stanley's "Hard Times." D tuning is more commonly used by old-time pickers. Listen to Pete Steele's "Coal Creek March," Snuffy Jenkins' "Lonesome Road Blues," and Ola Belle Reed's "Boat's Up the River."

34 SAWMILL TUNING

Also called "modal tuning" and "mountain minor," the sawmill tuning is an open G suspended chord, **gDGCD**, as heard on Track #4:

TRACK 4

Sawmill Tuning:

5 = G

4 = D

3 = G

2 = C

1 = D

It's exactly the same as G tuning, except for the second/B string, which is tuned up to C. The songs played in sawmill tuning have a very haunting and bluesy sound, as the scale employed has a ♭7th and ♭3rd, just like the blues scale. The tuning is a signature sound of Appalachian music; in fact, the term "high lonesome sound," now often associated with bluegrass, was coined by folk musician John Cohen in his 1963 film that documented the music of Appalachia. The film featured Roscoe Holcomb, who often used the sawmill tuning.

Some well-known songs usually played in this tuning include "Pretty Polly," "Little Sadie," "The Cuckoo," "East Virginia," "Cold Rain and Snow" (adapted to the rock genre by the Grateful Dead in the mid-1960s), "Cluck Old Hen," and "Shady Grove." These songs are well over a century old. They probably originated in the British Isles and were re-worked by Appalachian pickers. On the next page is a sample of "Pretty Polly," played clawhammer style, so you can hear the flavor of the sawmill tuning. It's all one chord. (See Tip #46 for more on clawhammer technique and Tip #75 for info on reading tablature.)

Pretty Polly

Sawmill tuning (gDGCD)

clawhammer style

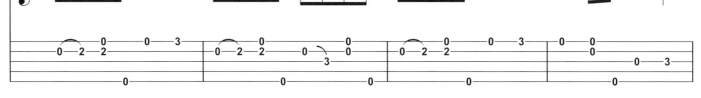

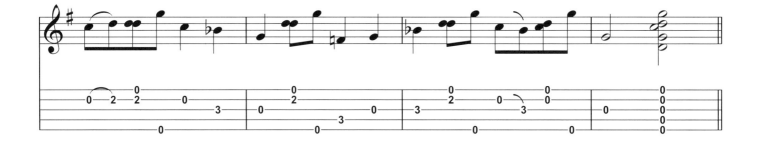

Most "modal" tunes, as many people call them, are one- or two-chord songs,
and the other chord (besides the open Gsus4) is an F6/9 chord, played like this:

F^6_9

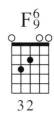

32

38

35 C TUNING

Old-time pickers often use the C tuning, and it was pretty much the standard tuning during the late 1950s and early 1960s folk era (see Tip #95). In his 1948 banjo instruction book, Pete Seeger called it the "standard tuning," though he offered some songs in other tunings. In subsequent editions of the book (still in print today!), he mentions that if he were to update the book, he would offer the G tuning as the most popular, standard tuning. Earl Scruggs recorded several songs in C tuning, including "Farewell Blues," "Home, Sweet Home," and a variant of "Soldier's Joy."

Unlike G tuning, C tuning does not tune your banjo to an open chord, C or otherwise. It's the same as G tuning, with the fourth string lowered to C: **gCGBD** (listen to Track #5):

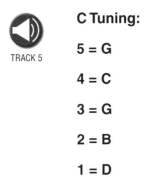

TRACK 5

C Tuning:

5 = G

4 = C

3 = G

2 = B

1 = D

The chord shapes you learned for G tuning are still useful in C tuning, if you adjust for the lowered fourth string. Sometimes you have to raise the fourth string two frets (as in the G chord, below), but for some chords, the fourth string stays open. And when you play in the key of C, you have a wonderful bass fourth string/C note:

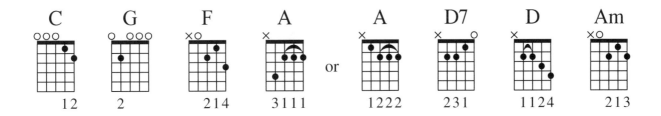

C tuning is a variant of the first documented five-string banjo tuning. The oldest banjo instructional book, Gumbo Chaff's *Complete Preceptor for the Banjo* (1851), offers an F tuning (cFCEG), which can be thought of as the C tuning but seven frets lower. Around the end of the 1800s, gut-string classical banjo players played in C tuning as we know it (gCGBD), though some of the music appears to have been written for G tuning (see Tip #30).

For some old-time samples of C tuning, listen to Buell Kazee's "Black Jack Davy," Hobart Smith's "Cindy," or Pete Seeger's "Cumberland Mountain Bear Chase."

The C tuning (minus the fifth string) is also standard tuning for the plectrum, four-string banjo.

Double C is often used by old-time pickers. It's just like C tuning, except the second string/B is tuned up to a C note, giving you a Csus2 chord: **gCGCD**, as heard on Track #6.

Double C Tuning:

TRACK 6

5 = G

4 = C

3 = G

2 = C

1 = D

If you fret the first string at fret 2, you have a C major chord:

C

Capoed up two frets, with the fifth string also tuned up two frets, this tuning is often used to play key-of-D fiddle tunes. Many contemporary old-time pickers use double C to play songs that used to be played (on older recordings) in C tuning.

As in the sawmill tuning, many songs played in double C are one-chord songs, or have only the barest suggestion of another chord. Here's a little bit of the classic fiddle tune, "Johnson Boys," played in this tuning. Most players would capo up two frets and tune the fifth string up to A, but it's played in double C here, with no capo or re-tuning. (See Tip #46 for more on clawhammer technique and Tip #75 for info on reading tablature.)

TRACK 6
(cont.)

Johnson Boys

Double C tuning (gCGCD)

37 DSUS AND D7SUS TUNING

Dock Boggs often used a Dsus tuning, which has an eerie sound very similar to the sawmill tuning (also a suspended chord). The notes are **f♯DGAD**, as heard on Track #7:

TRACK 7

Dsus Tuning:

5 = F♯

4 = D

3 = G

2 = A

1 = D

You'll hear Dsus on Boggs' "Danville Girl" and "Pretty Polly," although he is often tuned a whole step or half step lower than usual. All the sawmill tunes can be played in this tuning if the Gsus4 chord doesn't suit your vocal range.

Boggs and other old-time players also used a variant of Dsus. By de-tuning the fourth string, he created a D7sus4 chord (even spookier than Dsus) and used it on "Oh Death," "Prodigal Son," and other tunes. The tuning is **f♯CGAD** (also heard on Track #7):

TRACK 7
(cont.)

D7sus Tuning:

5 = F♯

4 = C

3 = G

2 = A

1 = D

In addition to giving you the bluesy, ♭7th sound, the low C/fourth string lets you play a lower melody note. You'll hear that low note in the 4th string hammer-on lick in the following version of the old folk tune, "Shady Grove."

Shady Grove

D7sus tuning (f♯CGAD)

If you raise the D string a whole step while in double C tuning, you have an open C chord—**gCGCE** (as heard on Track #8):

Open C Tuning:

5 = G

4 = C

3 = G

2 = C

1 = E

Uncle Dave Macon used this tuning for "Way Down the Old Plank Road," "Rise When the Rooster Crows," and many other songs. Also listen to Dock Boggs' "Little Omie Wise" (a famous murder ballad), Taj Mahal's "Colored Aristocracy," Frank Proffitt's "I'll Never Get Drunk Anymore," and Roscoe Holcomb's "Black Eyed Susie."

Tuned or capoed up two frets, this is an excellent tuning for key-of-D fiddle tunes. Here are the F, G, and G7 chord shapes:

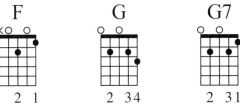

39 FRETTING HAND MANEUVERS

Usually, you pick strings with the picking hand. But the fretting hand can also sound notes by performing *slides*, *hammer-ons*, *pull-offs*, and *bends*.

- A *slide* from one fret to another is represented in notation by a line connecting the two notes (the starting and ending points of the slide). Sometimes you slide up to a fret from one or two frets back, or play a note and then slide down quickly to no specific fret. Always keep the string firmly pressed down to the fretboard while sliding.

- Sometimes you sound a note by striking the fret suddenly with a fretting finger (instead of plucking it with your picking hand). This is called *hammering on*. You can hammer onto an open string or a fretted string. Melodic clawhammer pickers sometimes hammer onto a string other than the one they just picked (for example, pick the open second string and hammer onto the third string/2nd fret).

- You can sound a note by plucking a string downward with your fretting finger. It's called a *pull-off*, which you can do to an open string or a fretted string. You can also pull off of a string other than the string you just picked; for example, pick the open second string and pull off the first string/2nd fret.

- When you *bend* a note, you fret it and stretch it up or down with the fretting finger (towards the ceiling or floor) to raise the pitch. Bends can create a bluesy effect.

Here's how all these maneuvers look in tab and how they sound (see Tip #75 for more on tablature):

TRACK 9

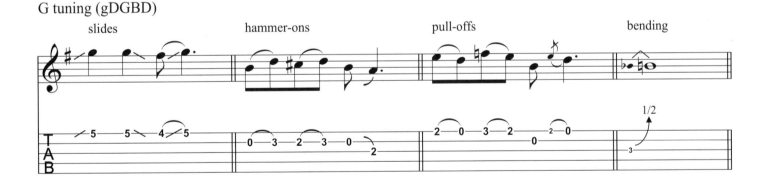

40 THE G MAJOR SCALE

When you play in G tuning, in the key of G, it's good to know the G major scale, because that's where you'll find most of your melody notes. In fact, if you play the first position G major scale written below—dozens of times and keeping a steady rhythm—soon you'll be able to find melodies without hunting for the notes; they'll just come to you. Try it: practice this scale for a few minutes, then try to pick out familiar tunes like "Happy Birthday," "Twinkle, Twinkle Little Star," and other tunes you've known since childhood.

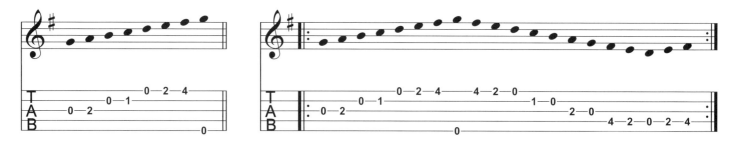

Whether you play clawhammer style, bluegrass style, or any style in which you pick out a melody, the G major scale will help you. Once you can find the melody notes, you can embellish them or fill them out with rolls (Tip #53), the clawhammer strum (Tip #46), or with double thumbing (Tip #51).

41 THE C MAJOR SCALE

If you're playing in the key of C, in G tuning, become familiar with the following C major scale; it will help you pick out melodies. It contains all the same notes as the G major scale (Tip #40), except there's an F instead of an F♯:

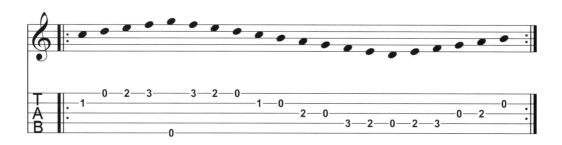

After practicing the C major scale, try to pick out melodies like "This Land Is Your Land," "Yankee Doodle," or "I've Been Working on the Railroad."

42 MOVEABLE CHORD SHAPES/ SCALES

In G tuning, there are three chord shapes that include no open (unfretted) strings, so they can be played all over the fretboard.

For example, the barred A chord is moveable, and you can play it all over the neck to make different chords (*barring* involves fretting two or more strings simultaneously with one finger).

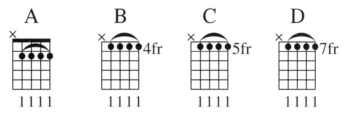

The F chord shape is also moveable.

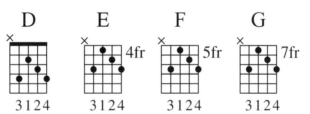

The D chord shape is also moveable.

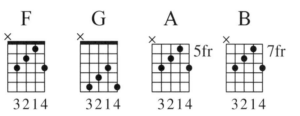

There are moveable major scales that relate to these three chord shapes:

- Before playing one of the major scales, play the related chord shape (barre, D, or F shape). The notes in that chord shape are major scale notes.

- As you play the scale, you can move your hand off the chord shape to play adjacent major scale notes. Keep coming back to the chord shape as a reference point.

- Play each scale over and over until you can play it automatically without thinking about it. Each one is a loop that keeps repeating.

- Move each scale up the neck. If you play the barre A scale a fret higher, it's a B♭ scale. If you move the F shape/G major scale two frets higher, it's an A scale, and so on.

- Try picking out some melodies, as you did with first position major scales in Tips #40 and #41.

Barre

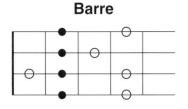

A major scale/barre

F Shape

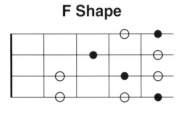

G major scale/F shape

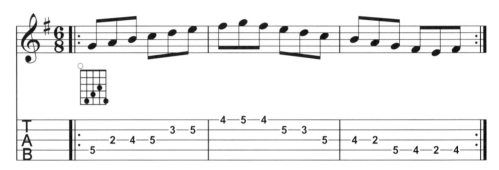

D Shape

D major scale/D shape

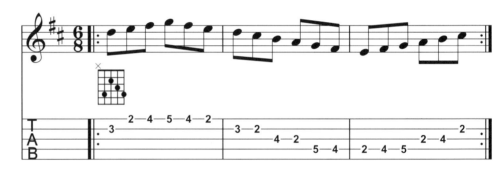

43 PLAY THE BLUES!

The ♭3rd, ♭7th, and ♭5th are *blue notes*, i.e., they're not found in the major scale. If you sprinkle them into your ad-lib melody playing, they'll impart a bluesy feel. Here are the blue notes in the G and C major scales (in G tuning):

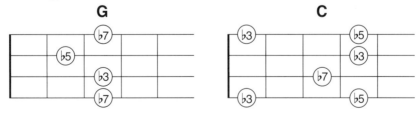

You can also add blue notes to the moveable major scales:

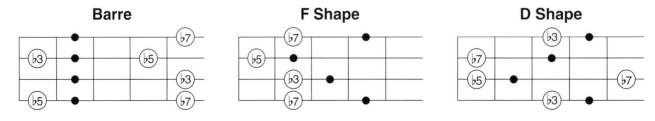

Here's how to "bluesify" a simple melody using the old folk tune, "Nine Pound Hammer." In the music notation and tab below, and on the recording, the basic melody is played, clawhammer style, during the first eight bars. The next eight show how to mix in blue notes. (See Tip #46 for more on clawhammer technique and Tip #75 for info on reading tablature.)

TRACK 10

Nine Pound Hammer

G tuning (gDGBD)

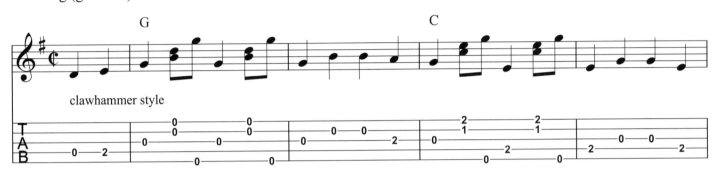

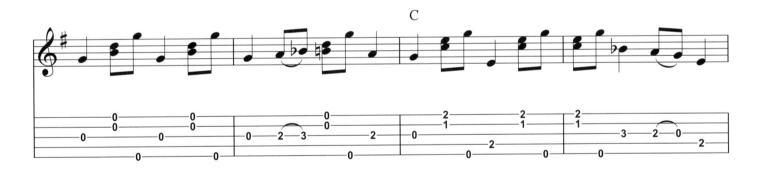

HARMONICS!

If you touch a string at certain strategic frets, instead of fretting it the usual way, plucking the string will create a bell-like chime known as a *harmonic*. The easiest place to get harmonics is at the 12th fret; the 7th and 5th frets are the next easiest spots.

- To get harmonics, you have to touch the string (don't push it down to the fretboard) right over the fretwire—not between fretwires as you do when fretting a string.

- To get that bell-like tone, take the fretting finger off the string right after you pluck it.

- The harmonics at the 12th fret are the same notes you get when you fret the strings at the 12th fret; they are an octave higher than the open string.

- Harmonics at the 5th fret are not the same as the fretted notes at the 5th fret. They are the same as the open strings, but two octaves higher.

- Harmonics at the 7th fret are the same notes you get when you fret the strings at the 7th fret, but an octave higher.

- You can strum a whole "chord" harmonic, by barring (but just lightly touching) all four strings at once at the 12th, 7th, or 5th fret.

Physicists know that the strategic harmonic spots on banjo (or any stringed instrument) are not random. The 12th fret is halfway between the nut and the bridge; the 5th fret is a fourth of the way; and the 7th fret is a third of the way up the neck.

Harmonics can be played on any stringed instrument; they've been used as a pretty effect for centuries in music of all types. Scruggs used harmonics in "Bugle Call Rag" and "Foggy Mountain Chimes," and pickers often use harmonics in the old song, "Grandfather's Clock," to imitate a clock chiming.

TRACK 11

G tuning (gDGBD)

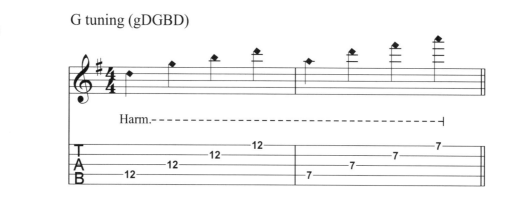

45 DIMINISHED AND AUGMENTED CHORDS

A diminished seventh chord is composed of four notes, and it can be named after any of the four. The name you give it depends on its context within a tune. Diminished seventh chords are written like this: Cdim7 or C°7.

Here are some moveable diminished seventh chord shapes and first-position diminished chords:

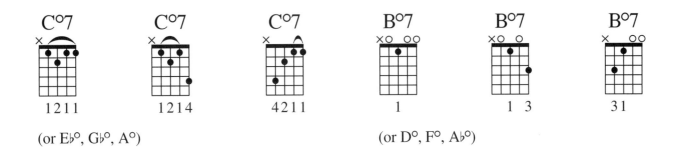

(or E♭°, G♭°, A°)   (or D°, F°, A♭°)

Diminished chords repeat every three frets:

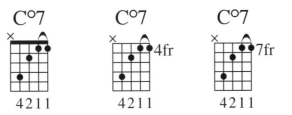

An augmented chord is a major chord with a ♯5th. Augmented chords repeat, too. Move an augmented chord shape up four frets, and you get the same chord with a different voicing. If you raise the interval of the 5th in any of the three moveable major chord shapes (see Tip #42), you get the same as an augmented shape:

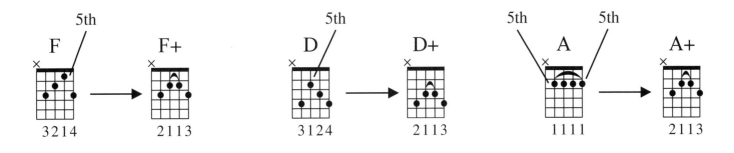

CLAWHAMMER (FRAILING)

The clawhammer strum, also called "frailing" the banjo, comes from Africa. Minstrel banjo is based on it, and so is a good deal of old-time banjo picking. It's a down-picking style; here's the basic strum:

- Pick down on a single note, such as the first string, with the back of the fingernail of your index or middle finger.

- Brush down with the same finger (or another finger) on the treble strings (the first and second, or the first, second, and third).

- Pick down on the fifth string with your thumb.

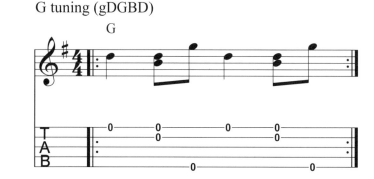

You can add hammer-ons, pull-offs, and slides for embellishment:

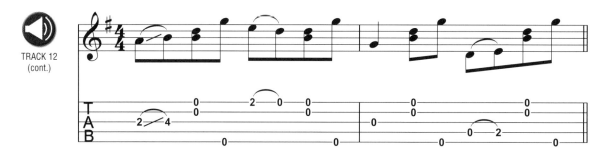

You can also play the melody of a song by down-picking with the index or middle finger, and then filling in the gaps between melody notes, when they occur, with the downstroke on the treble strings and the fifth string. Sometimes you may have to sacrifice a melody note in order to keep the rhythm rolling. For example, here's "Twinkle, Twinkle Little Star" in the key of G, clawhammer style:

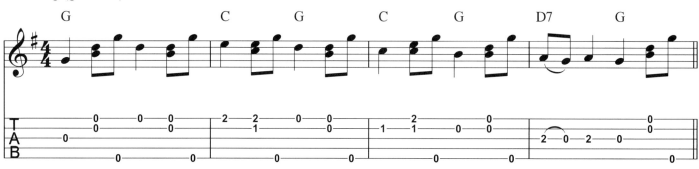

47 WHERE TO STRUM

The sound of your banjo changes depending on where you strum it. You get a bright, trebly sound when you strum near the bridge and a mellower sound when you strum where the pot meets the neck. Seasoned players use these nuances to add dynamics and color to their music. Experiment!

48 MOVEABLE MINOR CHORDS

By shifting one or two fingers around, you can make the moveable major chords (the barre, D shape, and F shape) into minor chords.

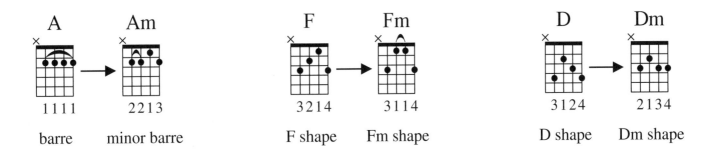

If you combine this knowledge (how to make major chords minor) with the F–D–Barre roadmap (see Tip #84), you can play any minor chord in several places on the fretboard, as high or low as you please. For example, here are all the Fm chords:

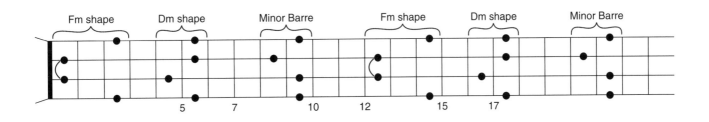

49 MOVEABLE 7TH CHORDS

It only takes a slight shift to make any moveable major chord a seventh chord:

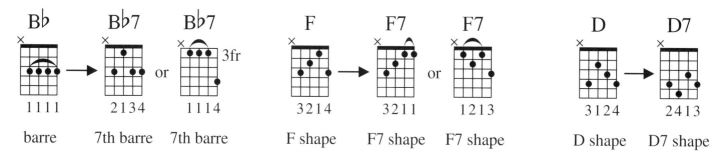

| Bb | Bb7 | Bb7 | F | F7 | F7 | D | D7 |
| barre | 7th barre | 7th barre | F shape | F7 shape | F7 shape | D shape | D7 shape |

Combining your knowledge of moveable seventh chords with the F–D–Barre roadmap (see Tip #84) allows you to play any seventh chord in at least three places on the fretboard. Here are all the F7s:

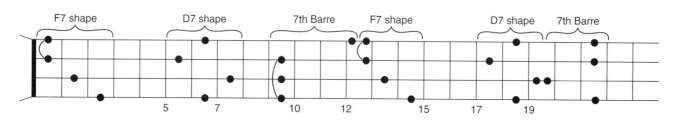

50 LEARN ALL THE G AND C CHORDS

When you're tuned to open G, the keys of G and C are the easiest keys. One practical way to begin learning chords up the neck is to memorize all the G and C chords. The fretboard diagram below will help you memorize all the G chords. Strum or pick a bar of each, keeping a steady rhythm, while ascending the fretboard:

All the G Chords:

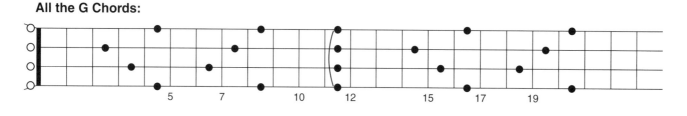

Locate other chords in relation to the G chords. For example, F is two frets below G, and A is two frets above G:

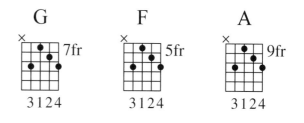

| G | F | A |
| 3 1 2 4 | 3 1 2 4 | 3 1 2 4 |

The following diagram will help you learn all the C chords.

All the C Chords:

Strum or pick a bar of each C chord, ascending the fretboard, as you did with the G chords. Then locate other chords in relation to the C chords. For example, B is one fret below C, and D is two frets above C:

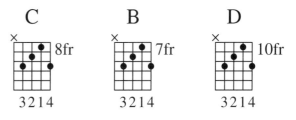

51 DOUBLE THUMBING/ DROP THUMBING

Fiddle tunes are an important part of the repertoire of old-time banjo players. There are 150-year-old tunes every five-string picker needs to know, and folks are always writing new ones. *Double thumbing* and *drop thumbing* are picking-hand maneuvers that make clawhammer solos subtler and enable you to more fully render a fiddle tune without sacrificing melody notes to the clawhammer style.

Double thumbing involves playing the fifth string with your thumb, between melody notes, as filler to keep the rhythm moving along. For instance, instead of playing the old fiddle tune "Old Joe Clark" this way (clawhammer style without double thumbing):

G tuning (gDGBD)

TRACK 13

clawhammer style

Add some double thumbing and listen to the difference:

G tuning (gDGBD)

TRACK 13
(cont.)

Drop thumbing involves dropping your thumb down to pick grace notes (filler notes) between melody notes. The drop-thumb notes can also be melody notes. Here's "Old Joe Clark" with drop thumbing (the "T" in the notation stands for "thumb"):

G tuning (gDGBD)

TRACK 13
(cont.)

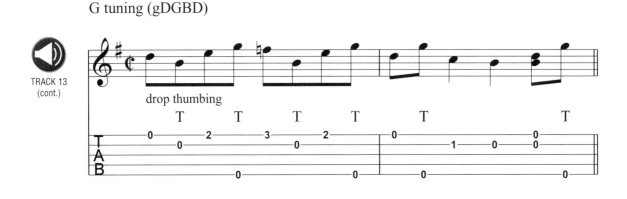

52 TWO-FINGER PICKING

Besides playing clawhammer style, many old-time banjo players pick with the thumb and one finger. This is called *two-finger picking*. Sometimes it can sound primitive compared to Scruggs-style picking, but it's a great sound, and in the hands of some experts it approaches the sound of three-finger rolls.

There are two types of two-finger picking, though many players combine the two within a song:

Thumb Lead

- The thumb plays melody notes.

- The index finger fills in with first- or second-string notes.

- Sometimes, to fill more space, you play the fifth string with your thumb followed quickly by the first string.

For example, here's a two-finger version of "Nine Pound Hammer" (see Tip #43), with the thumb leading:

Nine Pound Hammer

G tuning (gDGBD)

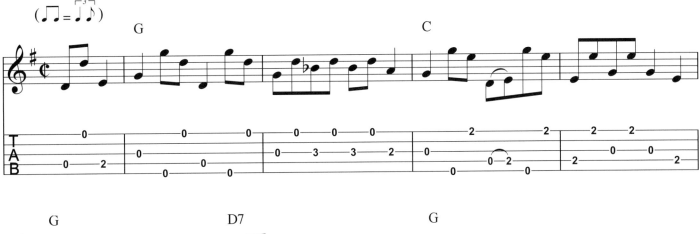

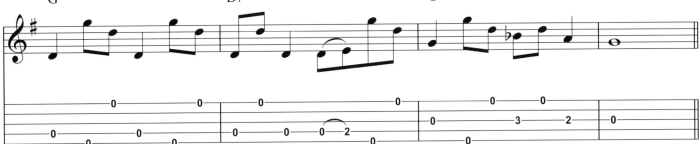

Index Lead

Thumb-lead works well when a song's melody notes are mostly on the lower strings. If a good deal of melody is on the first and second strings, index-finger lead is easier.

- The index finger plays melody notes.

- The thumb plays fill-in notes on the fifth string.

- To fill in longer spaces between melody notes, the thumb drops down and picks the string below the melody note.

- Then the finger repeats the melody note, and the thumb picks the fifth string.

In the example below, the basic melody to the chorus of "Buffalo Gals" is embellished with index finger-lead, two-finger picking.

TRACK 15

Buffalo Gals

G tuning (gDGBD)

See Tip #91 for a list of two-finger banjo pickers of renown.

53 THREE-FINGER ROLLS

They call bluegrass banjo rolls "three-finger rolls," but they're actually played with the thumb and two fingers—the index and middle finger. Most pickers place their ring finger and little finger on the banjo head together, as shown in the photo, to brace the picking hand.

- The middle finger almost always picks the first string.

- The thumb picks strings 3, 4, 5, and sometimes 2.

- The index finger picks strings 2, 3, and 4.

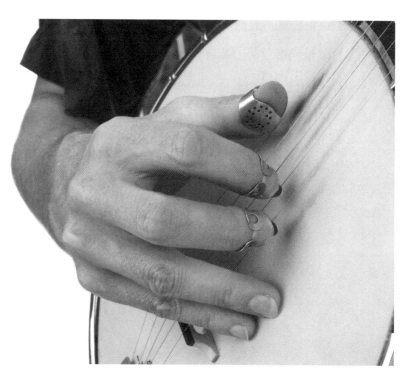

Every player needs to practice the following eight-beat rolls over and over until he/she can play them quickly and smoothly, using the picking fingers that are indicated by letters T (thumb), I (index), and M (middle):

TRACK 16

G tuning (gDGBD)

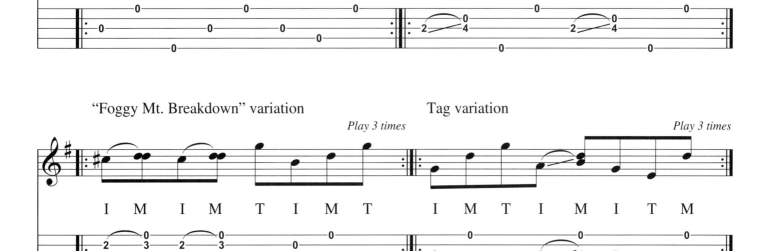

The last three rolls are variations of the basic rolls. They involve fret-hand slides, hammer-ons, or pull-offs (see Tip #39).

Whether you're playing accompaniment or solos, you mix up the rolls, seldom playing one roll over and over. When playing a solo, you make the melody, or at least a suggestion of it, fit into rolls. For example, here are the first eight bars of "Nine Pound Hammer" (see Tip #43), played with three-finger rolls:

TRACK 17

Nine Pound Hammer
(Three-Finger Style)

For more on how to use the rolls, see the Hal Leonard book *Complete Bluegrass Banjo* by Fred Sokolow.

54 SPEED

Whether it's a galloping clawhammer tune or a bluegrass instrumental in overdrive, the speed of banjo picking can be daunting for the novice player. Here are some tips on gaining speed:

- Play a clawhammer strum on an open chord (e.g., G, in G tuning) at a steady pace that's comfortable for you. Then gradually speed up, until you're going as fast as you can. Repeat this several times a day.

- If you're a bluegrass player, do the same with one of the basic patterns (see Tip #53).

- Do this same process, but now change chords every bar.

- You can practice your strums or picking patterns throughout the day, even when you're separated from your banjo, by drumming or strumming with your fingers on a desk or any surface.

- Have faith that it'll happen, but keep pushing the speed.

55 SINGLE-STRING PICKING

Don Reno and Eddie Adcock were early practitioners of this style, which involves playing rapid scale-based licks, alternating downstrokes with the thumb and upstrokes with the finger. The result sounds like flatpicking. Béla Fleck, who employs a good deal of single-string picking when he plays his original jazz pieces, took much inspiration from guitarist Al Di Meola, who plays with a flatpick. Single-string picking makes some of Di Meola's licks playable on the five-string.

Here are some samples of single-string picking. When playing any of these phrases, it's helpful to position your fretting hand in the chord shape that's indicated:

TRACK 18

G tuning (gDGBD)

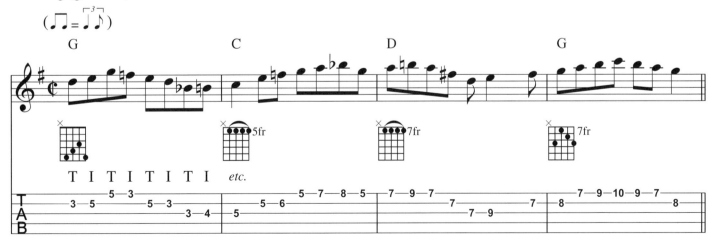

56 MELODIC PICKING

In the late 1950s and early 1960s, Bill Keith, Tommy Thompson, Eric Weissberg, and a few other banjo virtuosos began developing a style of picking that could be seamlessly interwoven with Scruggs picking. It was called *melodic style*, *chromatic style*, or *Keith style*, and it allowed banjo pickers to play fiddle tunes note-for-note, rather than in the stylized Scruggs fashion, which often compromises the melody in order to fit it into three-finger rolls. Melodic picking also made it possible to play major scale-based improvisations and bluesy cascades of notes that cannot be executed with rolls. This approach birthed a whole new style of improvisation on the banjo.

To begin to understand melodic picking, play the following licks and major scales. Notice the "overlapping note" method; you play a higher note by going lower on the fretboard, on a higher string, often mixing in open strings as well. The blues scale example involves fretting the high G string—see Tip #57 for more info on this.

TRACK 19

G tuning (gDGBD)

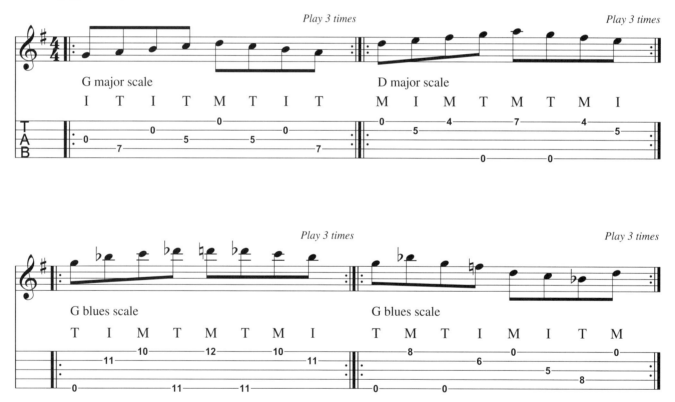

The following excerpt from "Turkey in the Straw" illustrates how melodic picking helps you adhere to the melody of many an old fiddle tune:

TRACK 20

Turkey in the Straw

G tuning (gDGBD)

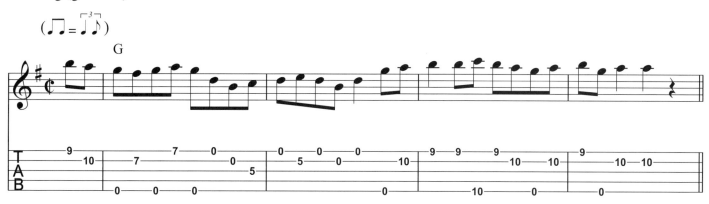

Butch Robins, Courtney Johnson, and others used melodic picking to play bluesy improvisations, while Pat Cloud adapted the style to create banjo arrangements of jazz and bebop solos. Béla Fleck employed it to play Paganini pieces and other classical music. Fred Sokolow and Bill Knopf both arranged several ragtime pieces making liberal use of the melodic style.

In the mid 1970s, several East Coast pickers like Ken Perlman, Bob Carlin, and Henry Sapoznik developed a melodic approach to clawhammer banjo. They combined melodic licks with double thumbing and drop thumbing (see Tip #51) and spearheaded a new banjo style—melodic clawhammer—in which fiddle tunes can be played on banjo without losing any of the melody notes. Here's a quick example of the style. It's an excerpt from the fiddle tune "The Eighth of January":

TRACK 21

G tuning (gDGBD)

57 FRETTING THE FIFTH STRING

In melodic and Scruggs-style picking, sometimes the fifth string is fretted. This can be done with a finger or with the thumb. For example, here are a Scruggs-style backup lick and a melodic lick. The grids show two ways to finger the chords ("T" stands for "thumb").

TRACK 22

G tuning (gDGBD)

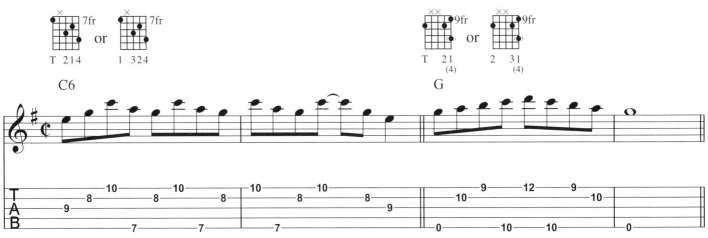

58 PLAYING WITHOUT A CAPO

Old-time banjo pickers almost always tune to the key in which they're playing. If a song is played in the key of D, they tune to D tuning (or D7, or D7sus). If it's in C, they tune to C tuning, double C, or open C. G tuning is used if a tune is played in the key of G. To play in other keys, they use a capo—G tuning, for example, capoed up two frets for the key of A, or C tuning capoed up four frets for the key of E, etc. Some pickers tune to C tuning and capo up two frets to play in the key of D. Of course, the 5th string is usually tuned up to match the capo (see Tip #27).

But bluegrass players sometimes follow Earl Scruggs' example and play in D, F, or E in G tuning without a capo. For example, to play in the keys of D or F, tune the fifth string up to A, and use these first position chords:

Key of D

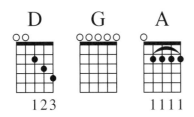

Key of F

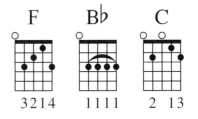

For the key of E, tune the fifth string up to B and use these chords:

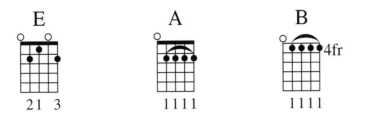

There are two main advantages to this approach:

- There's no time spent fumbling with capos.

- You don't lose the lower banjo notes.

PLAY WITH THE BEST BACKUP BANDS

Playing along with recorded music is an excellent way to practice. It's the next best thing to playing with other people, and it forces you into the rhythm groove and keeps you there. They don't have to be banjo recordings, however, using Flatt and Scruggs recordings as practice backup tracks is recommended. Here are some helpful tips:

- You have to know the song's key. (See Tip #32.)

- You have to know the chord changes. You can often find them online. (If they're in a different key than your recording, see Tip #83 on transposing.)

- Find the various "jam tracks" offered to students, featuring a band minus the banjo, for practicing purposes.

Start with very simple (two- or three-chord) songs that are played at a moderate or slow tempo. It pays off! This will prepare you for the next step: playing with other people.

60 LEARN COMPLETE SONGS

If you can play and sing a song from start to finish, you can lead other players in a jam session, serenade your significant other, sing your kids to sleep, enter competitions/talent shows/recitals, or launch your career. This means you'll have to:

- Memorize the words and the chord progression.

- Learn to play/sing the song without reading it!

- Practice a song by playing it all the way through over and over. Don't stop every time you make a mistake and start over again. Just keep playing and try to get it right the next time around.

- If one chord change in a song always trips you up, isolate that section and practice it separately.

It is very helpful to listen to a recording of a song you're trying to learn (by a performer you like) and sing and/or play along, over and over. Periodically, turn off the recording and perform the song by yourself. You'll discover the parts you tend to forget, and you can work on those specifically.

61 KEEP A STEADY TEMPO

Most people have a tendency to speed up during the easy parts of a tune and slow down for the hard parts. Not only is this unmusical sounding, it's bad practice!

- Keep to one steady tempo.

- Slow the whole song down to a tempo that allows you to keep a consistent beat. You can speed up gradually once you've ironed out the tough spots.

- Practice with a metronome (see Tip #18).

62 PLAY WITH OTHER PEOPLE

Once you've learned a handful of chords, some strums, and/or picking patterns, it's time to find some other, musically like-minded folks with which to jam. Playing music with others is a whole new experience! You'll discover your weaknesses and your strengths, but most of all, you'll be amazed how much fun it is to get in a solid rhythmic groove with a bunch of pickers. And, it's the fastest way to progress as a player.

A bluegrass banjoist needs a guitar player—someone who will sing and strum and let you solo every so often. An old-time or folk banjoist needs to play with a fiddler or guitar player—anyone who likes your kind of music, really. No matter what your musical genre, you can find people with a common interest to jam with. Ask your friends, family, and co-workers about other players (any instrument). When you get together with them, have some songs in mind that you can play well, try to find some tunes you both know, and be open to learning new ones. It's a one-of-a-kind experience!

There are free bluegrass, blues, old-time, and folk music jams meeting on a regular basis at private homes, restaurants, clubs, or music stores. Most jam groups are non-competitive, supportive, and non-threatening. A typical format is to sit in a circle and sing or play a tune together, taking turns soloing. When it's your turn to solo, you can decline if you're not comfortable; some people never solo in a jam session and just play backup, while others relish the opportunity to play solos.

Come to a jam with an open mind and a list of tunes you know, and don't worry about playing imperfectly or making mistakes. You're bound to learn something from just about every player you jam with, and that can be inspiring.

63 REPETITION GETS IT DONE

If a new chord, scale, or anything else you're trying to play is difficult at first, repeat it over and over, keeping a steady tempo. The great Indian master musician, Ali Akbar Khan, used to say (after teaching a student something new): "Now play it a hundred times." Eventually, the lick or scale becomes automatic and feels natural.

Practice a new chord in the context of a tune, or just switch from a familiar chord to the new one, over and over, in tempo. Sometimes two chords have one finger in common, so don't move that finger when switching from one chord to another. This common note makes the chord change easier and often results in a smoother sound.

 MAKE A WISH LIST (OF SONGS)

List the songs you'd like to learn to play and sing. This can include your all-time favorites—even the ones you may think are too difficult. As you learn them and check them off, you'll add them to your repertoire list (Tip #19). This is a good way to make sure you keep growing as a player.

 PRACTICE EVERY DAY

Even if it's only for ten or fifteen minutes, daily practice does more for you than two hours once a week. You're building physical skills and neural pathways. As with athletics, music requires daily exercise; you can't cram (like for a test) at the end of the week. Some people find it easiest to practice first thing in the morning, before all the daily business gets started. Others like to practice at night, after a workday, instead of watching television! You'll progress much faster on the banjo if you find a daily time that fits your schedule and practice at that time, every day.

 ORGANIZE YOUR PRACTICE

- Play the tunes you already know once through to warm up.

- Play the tunes you're currently working on.

- Practice some scales or common chord progressions, using moveable chords. (See Tips #41 and #42 for chords and scales.)

- Play randomly; discover something new on your banjo.

67 PRACTICE MENTALLY

You can practice without a banjo! If you're waiting in a line, on hold on the phone, or on a treadmill, you can visualize the banjo and go through songs, strumming chords or picking, mentally. Picture exactly where your fingers go and how the strumming or picking works. Visualizing chord positions and hand movements reinforces patterns.

68 ONE NEW CHORD A WEEK

If you learn just one chord a week, you'll have 52 new chords by the end of the year. Make sure you use your weekly new chord in a song. Find a chord chart for a song you've heard before, and if it includes one or two new chord shapes, learn to play it! When you can play a new chord in a song and get to it in time, you own it, and you'll be able to play it in any song. It's part of your vocabulary.

69 RECORD YOURSELF

There are many easy ways to do this with your computer, an iPhone/smart phone, or all kinds of inexpensive recording devices. You'll hear problems in your playing that you didn't know were there, but you may hear good things as well. Record yourself playing an entire tune from start to finish. Don't be discouraged if what you hear isn't perfect! Once you've spotted a flaw, whether it's a wrong note or irregular timing, work on it and re-record until it sounds better.

70 A SONG A WEEK

Learn a new song every week, and learn to play it from start to finish. This may mean learning a banjo solo, an instrumental version of the song, or it may mean learning to back yourself up (playing accompaniment) when you sing the song. Either way, by the end of the year, you'll have a sizable repertoire.

This is not as big of a challenge as it sounds. Thousands of well-known songs contain only two or three chords. You grew up hearing and singing many of them ("This Land Is Your Land," "Happy Birthday," "You Are My Sunshine," etc.), and it's fairly easy to learn to strum them on the banjo, play them clawhammer style, or play picking patterns while making the chord changes.

71 EXPAND BANJO CONSCIOUSNESS

Get outside your usual bag; it'll broaden your musical horizons. If you only play old-time songs, learn some bluegrass, or vice versa. For a bigger stretch, learn to strum or pick accompaniment to a new pop tune. If you've never played a jazz tune or a reggae tune, learn one. Learn a country standard (accompaniment, solo, or both). You'll find the chords in many songbooks. Here are a few suggestions for classic tunes of their genre:

Country:	"I'm So Lonesome I Could Cry"
Reggae:	"Three Little Birds"
Jazz:	"Georgia on My Mind"
Blues:	"Stormy Monday"
Bluegrass:	"Salty Dog Blues"
Old-Time:	"Way Down the Old Plank Road"
R&B:	"Stand by Me"
Swing:	"Fly Me to the Moon"
Rockabilly:	"It's So Easy to Fall in Love"
Tin Pan Alley : (early jazz/pop)	"There'll Be Some Changes Made"
Hawaiian:	"Sweet Leilani"
Grunge:	"Come as You Are"
Indie Rock:	"Miss Misery"

72 GET READY FOR SHOWTIME!

If you tell people you play banjo, they'll say, "Play me something!" (Or, more likely, "Can you play 'Dueling Banjos?'") Get a song up to performance level so that you'll be able to play it for them, or perform it at an open mic event. Enter it in a competition or put it up on YouTube. Conquer your stage fright and do one of those things! The threat of public scrutiny will make you work harder at really perfecting a tune—even if your "public" is one or two people in a living room.

To get a tune ready for performance, play it over and over, from start to finish. Don't stop for mistakes; just repeat it and get it right next time. Choose a song that's easy for you to play and sing—one you're comfortable with.

73 PRACTICE IN FRONT OF A TV

Many pros practice scales, licks, chord changes, strums, picking patterns, or anything that requires mindless repetition and muscle memory, while sitting in front of a silent TV. Your favorite nature programs are a good bet for this one. Anything that occupies your mind will do, because the mind just gets in the way.

74 YOU CAN PLAY ANYTHING

If a banjo arrangement is written out in tab (or music notation, if you read it), you can learn to play it, no matter how difficult it may seem. All you have to do is break it down into short musical phrases and learn them, one at a time, by repeating each phrase over and over, until your fingers "get it." Start playing each phrase with a slow enough tempo that you can play it with the right rhythmic feel; then gradually speed up.

TABLATURE

Also called *tab* for short, tablature is very popular among players of stringed/fretted instruments, because a beginner can learn to read it almost immediately. Tablature has been around since the Renaissance. Unlike standard music notation, tab tells the player which string to pluck and where to fret the string. Today, most banjo music is written in music and tab, or just tab.

- The five lines of banjo tablature represent the five strings. The bottom line is the fifth string, and the top line is the first string; it's as if you looked down at the fretboard while holding the banjo in playing position.

- Numbers on the lines represent frets. For example, a 3 on the top line tells you to play the first string at the 3rd fret.

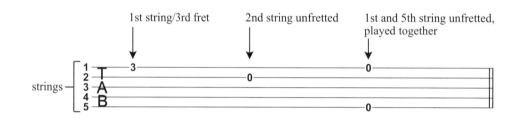

UP AND DOWN

"Up" is toward the bridge; "down" is toward the nut. Why? As you move up a string toward the bridge, you raise the pitch; when you move down a string, toward the nut, you lower the pitch. So, if you're playing an A chord by barring the 2nd fret, and you're told to "move it up two frets to play a B," then you barre the 4th fret.

WHERE THE NOTES ARE

You can play banjo all your life without knowing the names of the notes you're playing. Pete Seeger often quoted an old gag where a fellow asks the banjo player "Do you read music?" And he responds, "Not enough to hurt my playing." Though most banjo styles heard today are part of an aural tradition, there are many situations in which it would be helpful to know how to read music, or at least know where the notes are. This chart shows the note positions:

G Tuning

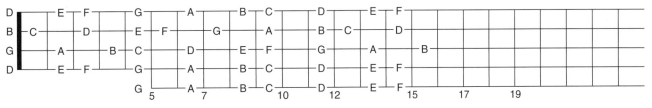

- Notice the spaces between many of the notes, with no letters (for example, the space between C and D on the second string). These are *sharps* and *flats*.

- Sharp means "a fret higher." C♯ (C sharp) is one fret above C.

- Flat means "a fret lower." D♭ (D flat) is one fret below D.

- Each of these "in-between" notes has two names. The note between C and D can be called C♯ or D♭.

- Notice that there are sharps or flats between most of the letter names (notes), but there is no sharp or flat between B and C or E and F.

Start by learning the notes in the first four or five frets, and your knowledge of notes on the fretboard will gradually creep up the neck as you continue to play.

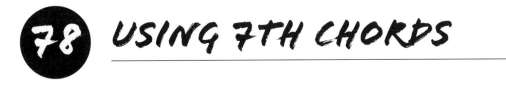

USING 7TH CHORDS

A seventh chord usually leads to the chord that is a 4th higher. For instance, G7 leads to C. If you're playing a G chord followed by a C, play a G7 before the C to give it a push in that direction. Try it and see!

A seventh chord is composed of these intervals: 1, 3, 5, ♭7. For example, C7 contains the 1st, 3rd, 5th, and ♭7th notes in the C major scale: C, E, G, and B♭. While major chords sound sunny and complete, and minor chords sound melancholy, seventh chords have a lot of tension, as if they're leading somewhere (up a 4th). They sound bluesy. In fact…

THE BLUES LOVES 7TH CHORDS

The rule in Tip #78 doesn't apply to the blues. In the blues, you often use seventh chords throughout instead of major chords, and they don't necessarily lead up a 4th. You can even end a blues on a seventh chord.

80 THE NUMBERS GAME

Musicians, pro and amateur, often use numbers rather than letters to name chords. At jam sessions, folks are just as likely to call out numbers ("go to the 4 chord") as letters ("go to the F chord").

The numbers refer to the major scale of a song's key. For example, in the key of C, a C chord is called the 1 chord. The second note in the C major scale is D, so if you're playing in the key of C, a D chord is called a 2 chord—whether it's D, Dm, D7, or any variation of D.

- Whatever key you're in, 1, 4, and 5 are the chords most often played. Countless blues, rock, country, folk, and bluegrass tunes use just these three chords.

- Use the "Circle of Fifths" chart (Tip #81) to identify the 1, 4, and 5 chords in any key, and become familiar with these "immediate chord families."

- You can become familiar with the sound of the 4 chord or the 5 chord. When you do, you're starting to understand the basis of music theory. You're figuring out how music works! Here's how to train your ear: take a simple, three-chord song that just contains the 1, 4, and 5 chords and write numbers under the letters. For example:

When the Saints Go Marching In

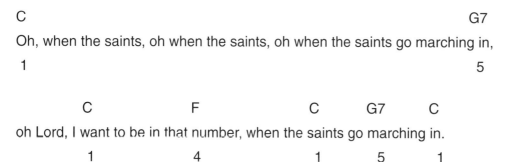

Play the song several times, being aware that when you change to G7, you're going to the 5 chord, and when you change to F, it's the 4 chord. Use the "Circle of Fifths" chart (Tip #81) to play the song in several different keys. (See Tip #83 on Transposing.) Whatever key you're in, be aware when you're going to the 4 chord or the 5 chord.

It's helpful to know what 1, 4, and 5 are in any key, without having to stop and think about it. The following chart shows you what they are in several easy banjo keys:

1-4-5 Chord Family Chart

	1	4	5
Key of E	E	A	B
Key of A	A	D	E
Key of D	D	G	A
Key of G	G	C	D
Key of C	C	F	G
Key of F	F	B♭	C
Key of B♭	B♭	E♭	F

81 CIRCLE OF FIFTHS CHART

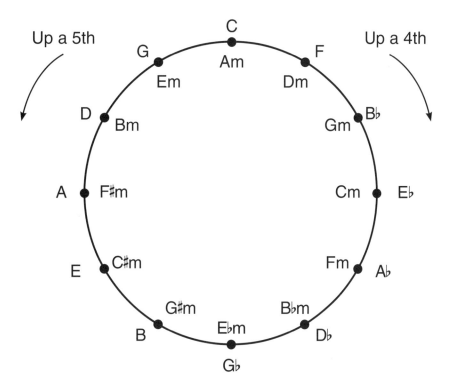

This chart groups chords in their 1–4–5 chord families. For example, if you look at C at the top of the chart, the note (or chord) that's a 4th above C is one step clockwise. The note (or chord) a 5th above C (or a 4th below) is one step counter-clockwise.

The same applies in any key. The chart says that, if you're in the key of E, the 4 chord is A (one step clockwise), and the 5 chord is B (one step counter-clockwise). Many songs have circle-of-fifths-type chord movement. For example, many songs start on the 1 chord and jump outside the chord family to a chord that is several steps counter-clockwise. Then they go clockwise, up by 4ths, to get back to the 1 chord. A song in the key of C may have this chord progression:

| C | A7 | D7 G7 | C ||

In this chord progression, you jump several steps counter-clockwise from C (the 1 chord) to A7. Then, using typical circle-of-fifths movement, you go clockwise (up a 4th) from A7 to D7, then up another 4th to G7, and up still another 4th to end back at C.

The chords inside the circle are *relative minors* (see Tip #82). Other uses of the circle of fifths (and other music theory involving scales, chord progressions, etc.) are explained in detail in Fred Sokolow's best-selling *Fretboard Roadmaps: 5-String Banjo* (Hal Leonard).

Every major chord has a *relative minor*, a closely related minor chord that is built on the sixth note of the major chord's scale. For example, the sixth note in the C major scale is A, so Am is the relative minor of C.

- Many songs include the relative minors of the 1 chord, the 4 chord, or the 5 chord—or any combination of them.

- Listen to the sound of a relative minor when it's played after the relative major chord. You've heard that chord change in a lot of popular songs, and now you can recognize it when you next hear it.

- Play a C and follow it with an Am. Do the same with a G and Em, and a D and Bm. Notice the similarities: no matter what key you're in, going from a major chord to its relative minor has an unmistakable sound.

- A shortcut: the relative minor is also three frets below the relative major. For instance, to find the relative minor of D, go three frets down from D (D♭, C, B); Bm is the relative minor of D.

Knowing how to immediately locate a relative minor chord can come in handy. Here's how you change each of the moveable major chord shapes into their relative minors:

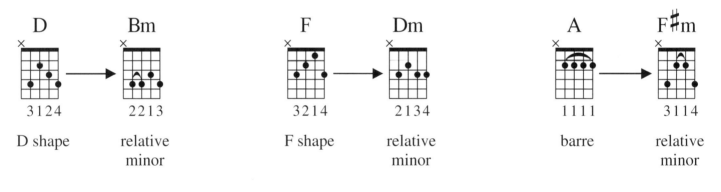

D	Bm	F	Dm	A	F♯m
3 1 2 4	2 2 1 3	3 2 1 4	2 1 3 4	1 1 1 1	3 1 1 4
D shape	relative minor	F shape	relative minor	barre	relative minor

83 *TRANSPOSING*

Transposing simply means changing keys. If a song you'd like to sing is written in a key that's too high or too low for your voice, you can transpose it to whatever key you like. You can change all the chords using the Circle of Fifths chart (Tip #81).

For example, if the song is written in D, and you can't quite reach the high notes, transpose it a whole step lower to the key of C. C is two steps clockwise from D on the circle, so all the chords in the tune must be changed two steps clockwise.

F–D–BARRE CHART

This chart, borrowed from Fred Sokolow's *Fretboard Roadmaps: Five-String Banjo*, shows how to find all the inversions (voicings) of any major chord, up and down the fretboard. All the F chords are shown below:

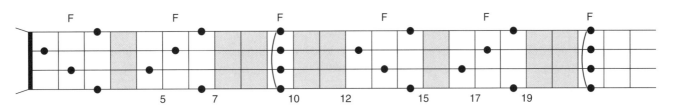

- Play the F shape/F chord.

- Skip a fret (4th fret) and play the D shape at the 5th fret. That's the next F chord.

- Skip two frets (the 8th and 9th) and play the barre at the 10th fret. That's the next F.

- Skip two frets (the 11th and 12th) and play the F shape at the 13th fret. That's the next F, and the cycle starts over (you began and ended with an F shape).

- It's an endless loop that keeps on going, until you run out of frets:

  ➡ F shape, skip one fret

  ➡ D shape, skip two frets

  ➡ Barre, skip two frets

  ➡ Start over with the F shape

You can start with any of the three shapes on any major chord. For example, here are all the A chords. It's the same pattern as above, starting at a different point in the loop:

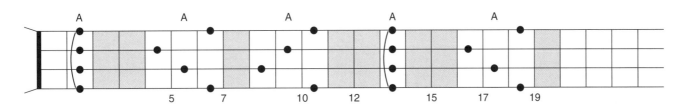

Practice the pattern by playing a steady strum or picking pattern and changing to a higher inversion every bar. In other words, climb the fretboard playing all the F chords, or all the A chords, or all the D chords, etc.

 85 DIFFERENT TEACHERS

Try out several teachers; each has a different approach and will give you different ideas. These could be flesh-and-blood teachers in your neighborhood music store, instructional books, video lessons, or cyber-teachers on the web. There are tons of instructional YouTube videos, for example. Try out as many as you can until you find an approach that suits your learning style best.

Some teachers only show you how to play specific songs or styles. Others stress technique, and still others emphasize music theory. This variety is beneficial, since you may have different needs at different times. Sometimes you just need to learn a certain song for your brother's wedding, and other times you want to learn how to play the blues on the banjo, strum chords higher up the neck, learn a new picking or strumming style, or understand jazzy chord progressions.

 86 LOOK, LISTEN, AND LEARN

Many people don't realize that when you're learning a new song or technique, *listening* is a major part of the process. In fact, it's the first step. If you listen to a song dozens of times before you even pick up the banjo to try and play the tune, you'll get much quicker results. Listen first; look at tab or music afterwards. Then you know how the tune is supposed to sound.

Listen to a lot of banjo players! And watch them in person and online. You'll see and hear new playing styles or techniques, you'll find new inspiration, and you'll discover songs you want to learn. And while we're on the subject…

 87 LEAVE IT OUT— AT ARM'S LENGTH

A banjo that's hanging on the wall, sitting on the couch, or resting on a stand in the living room or den will get played more often than the banjo that's locked up in a case. You'll progress more as a result. However, do take into consideration heat, cold, humidity (or lack thereof), earthquakes, and the worth of the instrument! Which brings us to…

Banjo Stands

If you're gigging a lot or switching between instruments, a banjo stand is a must. It's also a safe and handy way to display your banjo at home. Try to find one with the following features:

- Collapsible with an adjustable neck holder

- Some sort of locking mechanism

- A carrying bag

Most guitar stands can double as banjo stands.

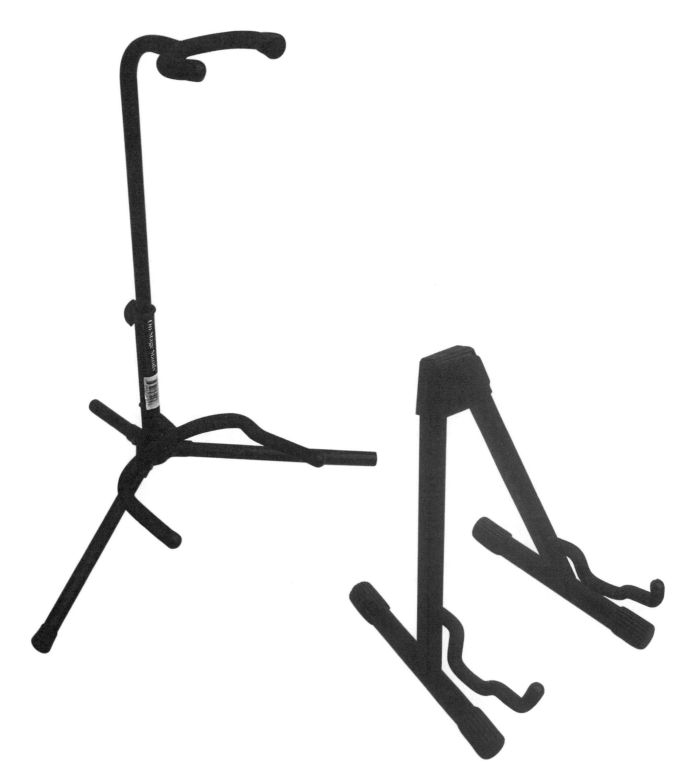

You can buy a variety of banjo (same as guitar) wall hangers that are mounted securely and look good. Hang up your whole banjo collection; it's better than a framed art print!

88 VISIT BANJO WEBSITES

There are many good banjo websites. They have free tutorials (both video and text), tablature for songs, blogs, and discussions about everything related to banjo, including maintenance, buying, and selling. Many of them announce banjo performances, seminars, classes, and other banjo-related events. They may help you find jamming partners as well (see Tip #62). There are sites specializing in minstrel banjo, old-time music, classical music, and just about anything you can imagine. Try **www.banjohangout.com** for openers.

89 GO TO A BANJO CONTEST

There are annual banjo/fiddle contests occurring throughout the year in many towns and cities all over the world. These events are fun! Usually, the prizes are not spectacular, but the experience is—whether you compete or not.

Most of the folks there are spectators. Contestants range from rank beginners to accomplished professionals—individuals and groups, so it's a good show! Plus, competing is a valuable experience, because you learn a lot by preparing a song and practicing it until you're comfortable performing it in front of an audience. And, if you practice a lot and performing still seems scary, overcoming that is a good experience too.

"Parking lot picking" is one of the main attractions at contests. Away from the competition stages, there are knots of pickers, happily playing and singing anywhere there is room for them. These people may be of any level, and you can get out your banjo, walk right in, join them, pick along, and it's free. You may even meet future jamming partners. You're liable to see and hear (and join) pickers of different genres: bluegrass, old-time, Western swing, acoustic jam bands, country music, minstrel, swing, etc.

There are often music-related crafts at the contests and performers putting on some good shows, folk dancing lessons, and food!

If you do compete, here are some tips from someone who has judged at dozens of contests:

- Enter in the right category (beginner, intermediate, advanced). If the piece you're playing is advanced, but your performance is intermediate, you'll be judged less harshly in the intermediate category.

- Pick a tune you can play well, even if it's simple or many people play it, over a tune that's obscure or complicated that you can almost play well. And play it at a speed you're comfortable with. A simple piece played well is much more musical than a difficult piece played poorly.

- Don't take it too seriously! If you make a mistake (drop a beat, hit a wrong note), just grin and continue. The world keeps turning, and the audience isn't there to pick on you; they just want to see you having a good time and playing good music.

90 FESTIVALS AND CAMPS

There are annual bluegrass and old-time music festivals occurring globally throughout the year. Some are Americana-type festivals at which you'll hear old-time music, bluegrass, acoustic jam bands, and country bands. Just type in "Bluegrass Festivals" or "Old-Time Music Festivals" on your search engine and plan your next vacation.

- Check banjo websites for a festival or camp in or near your area. Some are overnight; some are a weekend long or longer.

- In addition to performances, many festivals include master classes conducted by performers and teachers. You can pick up all kinds of playing tips from some of your favorite artists.

- At these events, you're surrounded by other fans of the instrument and of acoustic music, so they're always a fun and learning experience.

- "Parking lot picking" usually takes place at festivals too and is one of the main attractions.

Music camps are all about *instruction* and *jamming*.

- There are banjo camps, bluegrass camps, old-time music camps, and acoustic music camps. You can take group or private lessons on all kinds of subjects from a variety of teachers.

- There will also be group play-alongs/sing-alongs and performances by the instructors and the students. Plus impromptu jams of various sizes occupy all hours of the day and night.

- They're often held in beautiful, natural surroundings (cabins in the woods or on the beach).

91 KNOW YOUR BANJO MASTERS

Listen to the musical masters of the past and the virtuosos of the present to grow as a player. Now that music (and video) from about 1900 on is so accessible, it's easy and fun to do the research. Here are some five-string players whose recordings deserve your attention:

- **Minstrel Banjo**: Joe Ayers, Tim Twiss, Bob Flesher, Robert Winans, and Rob Mackillop have recordings and websites on which they re-create the minstrel music of the mid-19th century.

- **Ragtime Banjo**: Fred Van Eps, Vess Ossman, Gus Cannon, Clarke Buehling, Fred Sokolow, and Bill Knopf.

- **Classical Banjo**: William J. Ball, Geoff Freed (Black Tie Banjo), Béla Fleck, the New Criterion Banjo Orchestra, Douglas Back, and Elias Sibley.

- **Old-Time Banjo**:

  → **Clawhammer:** Grandpa Jones, Clarence Ashley, Rufus Crisp, Buell Kazee, Wade Ward, Lilly May Ledford (Coon Creek Girls), Ola Belle Reed, Fred Cockerham, Kyle Creed, Tommy Jarell, David Holt, Lee Sexton, Hobart Smith, Dock Walsh (Carolina Tar Heels), Frank Fairfield, Abigail Washburn (Uncle Earl, solo albums—she also melds old-time banjo with Chinese music!).

- ➡ **Melodic Clawhammer:** Ken Perlman, Bob Carlin, Mark Schatz, and Henry Sapoznik.

- ➡ **Two-Finger Picking:** (most of these players also played clawhammer style and/or three-finger picking): Dave Akeman (String Bean), Charlie Poole, Roscoe Holcomb, Snuffy Jenkins, Dock Boggs, Uncle Dave Macon, Mike Seeger, Wade Mainer, Obray Ramsey, Gus Cannon, Pete Steele, Bascom Lamar Lunsford.

- **Bluegrass Banjo**:

  - ➡ **Early**: Earl Scruggs (with Bill Monroe and with Flatt and Scruggs), Ralph Stanley (the Stanley Brothers), Don Reno (Reno and Smiley), Allen Shelton (Jim and Jesse McReynolds), J.D. Crowe (with Jimmy Martin and the New South), Sonny Osborne (the Osborne Brothers).

  - ➡ **Later**: Bill Keith, Doug Dillard (the Dillards), Eddie Adcock (the Country Gentlemen), Tony Trischka (Country Cooking and others), Alan Munde (Country Gazette), John Hartford, Courtney Johnson (Newgrass Revival), Béla Fleck, Alison Brown, Pat Cloud.

- **Folk Revival Banjo**: Pete Seeger (the Weavers and solo), Dave Guard (the Kingston Trio), Alex Hassilev (the Limeliters), Tommy Makem (the Clancy Brothers), Erik Darling (the Weavers).

92 RAGTIME AND CLASSICAL BANJO

In the 1860s, there was a movement to legitimize the five-sring for white urbanites and distance it from minstrel banjo. S.S. Stewart, a music publisher and banjo maker, was one of the leading advocates of what was called "guitar style" banjo playing, so called because, like much guitar playing, it was a three-finger, up-picking style, as opposed to clawhammer.

By the 1880s, this new banjo style had become extremely popular in the U.S. and England. The new practitioners played marches, popular tunes of the day, classical pieces, and operatic overtures. It was often called "classical style," and the repertoire frequently included classical music. Some virtuosos played first violin parts on the five-string, fronting orchestras. The players read from a musical score, wore no fingerpicks, and played gut strings on fretted banjos.

Sadly, none of the classical banjo era's virtuosos were recorded except for Vess Ossman and Fred Van Eps (father of the jazz guitarist, George Van Eps). Instead of recording classical repertoire, these two banjo masters recorded the popular music of the day, which was ragtime. The ragtime craze, which lasted almost up to the 1920s, included banjo players as well as pianists.

Today, there are numerous individuals and bands performing classical music on the five-string, gut-string banjo. Websites like **www.classicalbanjo.com** will apprise you of performers, concerts, recordings, songbooks, events, and organizations like the American Banjo Fraternity, all dedicated to the proliferation and preservation of the style. Béla Fleck recently recorded an amazing album of classical banjo music featuring duets with other classical virtuosos.

There is less ragtime five-string banjo activity, although Fred Sokolow and Bill Knopf both adapted rags to the banjo in the early 1980s, offering recordings and tablature books (some of which are still in print). Their arrangements incorporated melodic picking into older three-finger styles. Many recordings of vintage and contemporary ragtime banjo pickers are now available, and ragtime concerts occasionally feature banjoists.

93 OLD-TIME BANJO

"Old-time banjo" refers to banjo styles employed in "old-time music," a category invented by recording companies in the 1920s who needed to pigeonhole (and market) their releases of white, rural, Southern string band music. This included fiddle tunes, ballads, blues songs, gospel hymns, bawdy tunes, rags, and vaudeville numbers. Much of the repertoire was from oral tradition and too old to trace the composers.

The moniker stuck; today, there are old-time clubs, jam groups that meet regularly, websites, festivals, magazines, and of course, bands, concerts, and recordings. There is currently a resurgence of interest in old-time music among young people and a crop of musicians migrating from punk music to old-time.

Many old-time banjo pickers play clawhammer style, but some of the most famous old-time banjo pioneers were two- or three-finger pickers. Many employed all these techniques, sometimes combining two or more styles in a single song. See Tip #91 for more info on current and past old-time banjo pickers.

Frank Fairfield, a contemporary old-time musician, objects to classifications like "old-time" and "pop music." To paraphrase Frank, "Songs like 'Soldier's Joy' and 'Lonesome Road Blues' have been recorded and performed for centuries, by hundreds (maybe thousands) of artists, often by bands of many genres, like rock, country, cajun, blues, and Western swing. And they're still in circulation today. If that doesn't make them pop songs, what the heck is a pop song?"

94 BLUEGRASS BANJO

The fast, rolling, three-finger style picking made famous by Earl Scruggs is referred to as *bluegrass* banjo. Scruggs, along with Don Reno and a few other banjo pickers, mostly from North Carolina, pioneered the thumb-and-two-finger style of picking, more complex and syncopated than the thumb-and-one-finger style that preceded it. Both Scruggs and Reno were influenced by yet another North Carolina picker, Snuffy Jenkins, who played three-finger style in the 1930s.

Nearly every bluegrass banjo player, from the late 1940s to the present, bases his or her style on the playing of Earl Scruggs, both in overall approach to the instrument and in the playing of countless specific licks that came out of Scruggs's imagination. Many people associate the term "bluegrass banjo" with the sound heard on the most popular bluegrass tunes: "Foggy Mountain Breakdown," "Dueling Banjos," "Man of Constant Sorrow," and "The Ballad of Jed Clampett."

Typically, a bluegrass banjo has a resonator and tone ring. The Gibson Mastertone (especially pre-WWII Gibsons, such as the one Earl Scruggs played) used to be the gold standard. Today, many other banjo makers are very popular among pro bluegrassers, including Stelling, Deering, Wildwood, and OME.

In the 1970s, "newgrass" emerged, as bluegrass bands like Newgrass Revival and Seldom Scene blended traditional bluegrass with country, rock, and swing music. In more recent years, groups like Nickel Creek, Alison Krauss and Union Station, Béla Fleck and the Flecktones, and the Punch Brothers continue to push the boundaries of bluegrass by combining it with other musical forms.

95 FOLK REVIVAL BANJO

The baby boomer generation was introduced to the five-string banjo by the folk music boom of the late 1950s to early 1960s. This cultural phenomenon spawned the Newport Folk festival and other similar gatherings, as well as television programs like "Hootenanny," concerts, magazines, nightclubs, and coffee houses dedicated to the proliferation of folk music. It also brought rural, Southern folk musicians—and the banjo—to urban, collegiate audiences, popularizing old-time and bluegrass music nationwide.

Though many of the popular artists of this era were inspired by Harry Smith's *American Folk Music Anthology* and the raw banjo and guitar music of the South, most of them followed the lead of the 1940s folk group, the Weavers (featuring Pete Seeger on the five-string), and softened their music to make it palatable to urban audiences. Many of the popular groups of the folk music boom prominently featured the five-string, favoring the long-neck, Seeger-style banjo (see Tip #98).

Some of the more popular groups and banjoists of this era include:

- The Tarriers (Erik Darling on banjo), The Kingston Trio (Dave Guard), The Limeliters (Alex Hassilev), The Clancy Brothers with Tommy Makem (banjo), The Highwaymen, The Rooftop Singers, The New Christy Minstrels, and The Serendipity Singers.

Less commercial luminaries of the era include:

- The New Lost City Ramblers featuring Pete's half-brother Mike Seeger. This group (they all took turns playing banjo) exposed Northern city folks to very authentic mountain music.

- The Greenbriar Boys (Bob Yellin on banjo), who were one of the first non-Southern bluegrass bands.

Incidentally, a similar phenomenon, called "skiffle," happened simultaneously in England, encouraging teenagers like Jimmy Page, John Lennon, and Eric Clapton to learn to play music. Lennon's first instrument was the banjo!

Many people know that comedian Steve Martin began as a bluegrass banjoist performing at Disneyland and has resumed a career as a banjo player, performing at concert halls all over the U.S. It's noteworthy that, until Earl Scruggs joined Bill Monroe's band in 1945, banjo pickers in Southern string bands were often comedians. They wore funny outfits, like String Bean (Dave Akeman, who played with Bill Monroe before Scruggs) or Grandpa Jones, who had his grandpa schtick together when he was still in his twenties. Uncle Dave Macon, a Grand Ol' Opry regular, swung his banjo around while playing it, and whooped and hollered. Humor was part of the banjo gig. This trend stopped, post-Earl.

There's a story (probably true) that when Scruggs played his first solo at the Opry in Bill Monroe's band, Uncle Dave Macon and Grandpa Jones came out to the wings from backstage to see what all the fuss was about. The audience was going wild and making Earl repeat his solo over and over. They watched for a while, and then Uncle Dave said to Grandpa Jones, "He ain't one damn bit funny."

Grandpa Jones

David "Stringbean" Akeman   **Uncle Dave**

97 BANJO MAKERS

Some famous banjo makers of the late 19th century were Stewart, Vega, Fairbanks, Paramount, and Dobson. They made open-back banjos. The Vega and Fairbanks Whyte Lady banjos are highly prized, as are the Vega Tubaphone banjos.

In the early 20th century, some of the main names in banjo manufacturing were Ludwig, Orpheum, Gibson, and Bacon and Day. The Bacon and Day Silver Bell line was valued highly, as was the Gibson Mastertone. The Mastertone, from 1918 up to World War II, has long been considered the top-notch bluegrass banjo. Of course, it owes a good part of its mystique to the fact that Earl Scruggs played several pre-war Mastertones.

Gibson still makes banjos. Other contemporary banjo makers of note include Stelling (for bluegrassers), Wildwood, OME (formerly Ode), and Bart Reiter, who makes excellent open-backed banjos. Deering and Gold Tone both make all kinds of banjos; they are both well known for selling an entry-level banjo that is inexpensive and well made where it counts (good neck, good action, etc.). Deering, who bought the Vega line, makes a long-necked banjo exactly like the ones played in the folk era. They also make 6- and 12-string banjos.

Browse the Internet for greater and lesser banjo makers and to see some awesome banjos!

98 LONG NECK BANJOS

Pete Seeger invented the long neck banjo by slicing his banjo's neck in half and inserting three extra frets. Because it's longer, it can be tuned lower than usual—to an open E instead of an open G. Pete found that this enabled him to play comfortably in some keys that were difficult with the standard size banjo.

From 1948 to 1952, Pete played with the folk group, the Weavers. They had several commercial hits, preceding the folk boom by several years, and they were a model for most of the pop-folk groups that followed. Pete played the long neck banjo with the Weavers, providing the instrument high visibility. Vega began manufacturing a long neck, and it became the banjo of choice for urban folk groups like the Kingston Trio, the Limeliters, and many others.

The popularity of the long neck banjo faded with the tapering off of the folk boom, but in the 1980s, the Deering banjo company bought the name Vega and currently makes three long neck banjos, one of which has a Tubaphone tone ring and very closely duplicates the Vega long neck of the folk era. Greg Deering says that he decided to manufacture these banjos because "back in the day" of the folk boom, their sound and look inspired him to take up the instrument.

You need a special set of extra-long strings for long neck banjo.

With all due respect to the beloved Gene Autry and Roy Rogers, it appears that banjo—not guitar—was the instrument of choice for cowboys. Paintings, photographs, and written accounts all tell the same story. Besides, it's just common sense:

- Until the end of the 19th century, when the Sears, Roebuck and Co. catalog offered a guitar the workingman could afford, guitars were exclusively for the gentleman or lady of leisure.

- A banjo, especially the Civil War era, metal-rim banjo, is much more durable and suitable to life outdoors on the range than a wooden guitar. Banjos are louder, too.

100 WHY SO MANY TUNINGS?

One reason for all the bad jokes about banjos never being in tune: banjo players re-tune quite often, sometimes with each song.

- The fifth string, being a drone string that is seldom fretted, sounds best when it is tuned to a note in the tonic chord in the key of which you are playing. If you're playing in the key of E, you want an E, B, or a G♯ note to ring out over all the chord changes, because those are the notes in an E chord. So, whenever you sing two songs in a row, there's a good chance you'll have to retune the fifth string (unless they're both in the same key).

- Bluegrass players usually play in G tuning, but they still need to retune the fifth string when playing in keys other than G or C.

Old-time banjo pickers use multiple tunings and usually learn each song in a particular tuning of their choice. Here are the factors that determine the best tuning for a song:

- In what key do you want to sing it? Or, if it's a traditional fiddle tune, in what key must it be? Because of tradition, most fiddlers and banjo players are very particular about playing certain songs in certain keys.

- Which tuning will allow you to play the melody using the most open strings? The more unfretted strings, the easier the tune is to play, and the more of a droning, sustaining effect is created.

- Does the tuning fit the mood you want to create? Each tuning has a different personality. Open C has a bright, cheery sound, but D tuning has been called the "graveyard" tuning. Sawmill and Dsus have dark, spooky sounds as well. Double C is fairly bright, but with a modal touch.

Besides the tunings described in this book (G, C, double C, open C, D, Dsus, D7sus, and Gsus [sawmill]), there are many variations of all these. For example, Rufus Crisp played "Shady Grove" in a variant of sawmill, tuning the fourth string down to F, creating a G7sus tuning (gFGCD). Stu Jamison says Uncle Dave Macon played "Cumberland Mountain Deer Chase" in open C, but with the fifth string raised to A: aCGCE. Some people play in open D tuning with the fifth string tuned up to A instead of down to F♯. And there are minor tunings and tunings in which the fifth string is not part of the open chord. You can make up your own banjo tunings!

101 BANJO IN POP MUSIC

Once in a while, the five-string appears on the pop charts.

- It's front and center in the two instrumentals that became pop tunes after appearing in hit films: "Dueling Banjos" (*Deliverance*) and "Foggy Mountain Breakdown" (*Bonnie and Clyde*), plus the vocal "Man of Constant Sorrow" (*O Brother, Where Art Thou?*). And, it's prominently featured in TV show theme songs "The Ballad of Jed Clampett" ("The Beverly Hillbillies") and "Petticoat Junction."

- It's in the background of many country-pop songs by the Dixie Chicks, who started out as a bluegrass band. Countless other country hits, past and present, feature banjo—both clawhammer and Scruggs-style.

- Banjo is featured in rock or pop recordings including "Rocky Top," Neil Young's "Old Man," the Eagles' "Take It Easy," and by artists such as Sufjan Stevens, Andrew Bird, Builders and the Butchers, Grateful Dead ("Cumberland Blues"), Aerosmith ("Kings and Queens"), Modest Mouse ("Satin in a Coffin"), REM ("I Believe"), Uncle Tupelo ("New Madrid"), Wilco ("Forget the Flowers"), and many more.

- Pop-country bands with an Americana or folk-rock edge feature the five-string banjo prominently: Mumford and Sons, the Avett Brothers, and Old Crow Medicine Show (with their mega-hit, "Wagon Wheel") are prime examples.